ANALYSING QUANTITATIVE SURVEY DATA

CW00521342

for BUSINESS *and* MANAGEMENT STUDENTS

SAGE was founded in 1965 by Sara Miller McCune to support the dissemination of usable knowledge by publishing innovative and high-quality research and teaching content. Today, we publish over 900 journals, including those of more than 400 learned societies, more than 800 new books per year, and a growing range of library products including archives, data, case studies, reports, and video. SAGE remains majority-owned by our founder, and after Sara's lifetime will become owned by a charitable trust that secures our continued independence.

Los Angeles | London | New Delhi | Singapore | Washington DC | Melbourne

ANALYSING QUANTITATIVE SURVEY DATA

for BUSINESS *and* MANAGEMENT STUDENTS

JEREMY DAWSON

Los Angeles | London | New Delhi
Singapore | Washington DC | Melbourne

Los Angeles | London | New Delhi
Singapore | Washington DC | Melbourne

SAGE Publications Ltd
1 Oliver's Yard
55 City Road
London EC1Y 1SP

SAGE Publications Inc.
2455 Teller Road
Thousand Oaks, California 91320

SAGE Publications India Pvt Ltd
B 1/I 1 Mohan Cooperative Industrial Area
Mathura Road
New Delhi 110 044

SAGE Publications Asia-Pacific Pte Ltd
3 Church Street
#10-04 Samsung Hub
Singapore 049483

Editor: Kirsty Smy
Editorial assistant: Lyndsay Aitken
Production editor: Sarah Cooke
Marketing manager: Catherine Slinn
Cover design: Francis Kenney
Typeset by: C&M Digitals (P) Ltd, Chennai, India
Printed and bound by CPI Group (UK) Ltd,
Croydon, CR0 4YY

© Jeremy Dawson 2017

First published 2017

Apart from any fair dealing for the purposes of research or
private study, or criticism or review, as permitted under the
Copyright, Designs and Patents Act, 1988, this publication
may be reproduced, stored or transmitted in any form, or by
any means, only with the prior permission in writing of the
publishers, or in the case of reprographic reproduction,
in accordance with the terms of licences issued by the
Copyright Licensing Agency. Enquiries concerning
reproduction outside those terms should be sent to
the publishers.

Series Editors' Introduction © Bill Lee, Mark N.K. Saunders
and Vadake K. Narayanan 2016

Library of Congress Control Number: 2016935698

British Library Cataloguing in Publication data

A catalogue record for this book is available from
the British Library

ISBN 978-1-47390-750-8
ISBN 978-1-47390-751-5 (pbk)

At SAGE we take sustainability seriously. Most of our products are printed in the UK using FSC papers and boards.
When we print overseas we ensure sustainable papers are used as measured by the PREPS grading system.
We undertake an annual audit to monitor our sustainability.

CONTENTS

EDITORS' INTRODUCTION TO THE *MASTERING BUSINESS RESEARCH METHODS* SERIES

Welcome to the *Mastering Business Research Methods* series. In recent years, there has been a great increase in the numbers of students reading Master's level degrees across the business and management disciplines. A great number of these students have to prepare a dissertation towards the end of their degree programme in a time-frame of three to four months. For many students, this takes place after their taught modules have finished and is expected to be an independent piece of work. While each student is supported in their dissertation or research project by an academic super-visor, the student will need to find out more detailed information about the method that he or she intends to use. Before starting their dissertations or research projects these students have usually been provided with little more than an overview across a wide range of methods as preparation for this often daunting task. If you are one such student, you are not alone. As university professors with a deep interest in research methods, we have provided this series of books to help students like you. Each book provides detailed information about a particular method to support you in your dis-sertation. We understand both what is involved in Master's level dissertations, and what help students need with regard to methods in order to excel when writing a dissertation. This series is the only one that is designed with the specific objective of helping Master's level students to undertake and prepare their dissertations.

Each book in our series is designed to provide sufficient knowledge about either a method of data collection or a method of data analysis, and each book is intended to be read by the student when undertaking particular stages of the research pro-cess, such as data collection or analysis. Each book is written in a clear way by highly respected authors who have considerable experience of teaching and writing about research methods. To help students find their way around each book, we have utilized a standard format, with each book having been organized into six chapters:

- **Chapter 1** introduces the method, considers how the method emerged for what purposes, and provides an outline of the remainder of the book.
- **Chapter 2** addresses the underlying philosophical assumptions that inform the uses of particular methods.
- **Chapter 3** discusses the components of the relevant method.
- **Chapter 4** considers the way in which the different components may be organized to use the method.
- **Chapter 5** provides examples of published studies that have used the method.
- **Chapter 6** concludes by reflecting on the strengths and weaknesses of that method.

We hope that reading your chosen books helps you in your dissertation.

Bill Lee, Mark N.K. Saunders and Vadake K. Narayanan

ABOUT THE SERIES EDITORS

Bill Lee, PhD is Professor of Accounting and Head of the Accounting and Financial Management Division at the University of Sheffield, UK. He has a long-standing interest in research methods and practice, in addition to his research into accounting and accountability issues. Bill's research has been published widely, including in: *Accounting Forum*, *British Accounting Review*, *Critical Perspectives on Accounting*, *Management Accounting Research*, *Omega* and *Work, Employment & Society*. His publications in the area of research methods and practice include the co-edited collections *The Real Life Guide to Accounting Research* and *Challenges and Controversies in Management Research*.

Mark N.K. Saunders, BA MSc PGCE PhD FCIPD is Professor of Business Research Methods at Birmingham Business School, University of Birmingham, UK. His research interests are research methods, in particular methods for understanding intra-organizational relationships; human resource aspects of the management of change, in particular trust within and between organizations; and small and medium-sized enterprises. Mark's research has been published in journals including *Journal of Small Business Management*, *Field Methods*, *Human Relations*, *Management Learning* and *Social Science and Medicine*. He has co-authored and co-edited a range of books including *Research Methods for Business Students* (currently in its sixth edition) and the *Handbook of Research Methods on Trust*.

Vadake K. Narayanan is the Associate Dean for Research, Director of the Center for Research Excellence and the Deloitte Touché Stubbs Professor of Strategy and Entrepreneurship in Drexel University, Philadelphia, Pennsylvania. His articles have appeared in leading professional journals such as *Academy of Management Journal*, *Academy of Management Review*, *Accounting Organizations and Society*, *Journal of Applied Psychology*, *Journal of Management*, *Journal of Management Studies*,

Management Information Systems Quarterly, *R&D Management* and *Strategic Management Journal*. Narayanan holds a bachelor's degree in mechanical engineering from the Indian Institute of Technology, Madras, a postgraduate degree in business administration from the Indian Institute of Management, Ahmedabad, and a PhD in business from the Graduate School of Business at the University of Pittsburgh, Pennsylvania.

ABOUT THE AUTHOR

Jeremy Dawson is a Professor of Health Management at the University of Sheffield, UK, working jointly between the Institute of Work Psychology (part of the Management School) and the School of Health and Related Research (ScHARR). He is a statistician by background, and teaches a wide variety of subjects in the fields of statistics and research methods, including leading a research methods module for 350 MSc students, and teaching regular workshops on advanced statistics for academics and PhD students both in Sheffield and elsewhere.

His research includes a range of topics in the areas of health services management and research methodology. He has led several large-scale projects in the NHS, and he ran the NHS national staff survey for its first five years between 2003 and 2007. Other research interests include team and organizational climate, and work group diversity. His methodological research areas include interpretation of interaction effects, measurement of diversity, development of questionnaire scales, analysis of incomplete team data and the effects of aggregation on relationships.

He has published over 40 papers in refereed academic journals, as well as two book chapters, and is currently completing the writing of a book on using SPSS for health researchers. He is an editorial board member of six journals, and an Associate Editor of the *Journal of Occupational and Organizational Psychology*. He is a member of the International Advisory Board for the Center for the Advancement of Research Methods and Analysis (CARMA).

ACKNOWLEDGEMENTS

IBM® SPSS® Statistics software and IBM SPSS Amos screen images are reprinted courtesy of International Business Machines Corporation, © International Business Machines Corporation. SPSS Inc. was acquired by IBM in October, 2009. IBM, the IBM logo, ibm.com, and SPSS are trademarks or registered trademarks of International Business Machines Corporation, registered in many jurisdictions worldwide. Other product and service names might be trademarks of IBM or other companies. A current list of IBM trademarks is available on the Web at 'IBM Copyright and trademark information' at www.ibm.com/legal/copytrade.shtml.

1

AN INTRODUCTION TO CLASSICAL TEST THEORY AND QUANTITATIVE SURVEY DATA

1.1 ABOUT THIS BOOK

This book covers types of analysis that apply predominantly to data gathered via quantitative surveys. It is intended for non-experts who may be conducting survey research for the first time – for example for a student dissertation. As such, it has relatively few details of the mathematical underpinning of these methods (although some are essential to aid understanding), and concentrates more on the key principles of when and how the analysis should be done, and how it can be interpreted.

Although this text covers all of the key issues specific to analysis of quantitative survey data using classical test theory, many aspects of a broader study may be covered elsewhere. In particular, most types of analysis that would be used to describe data, or to test hypotheses, are covered in another book in this series (Scherbaum and Shockley, 2015). However, it will cover aspects of analysing survey data that other basic guides to data analysis might miss – in particular, data cleaning, reliability analysis, exploratory factor analysis (EFA) and confirmatory factor analysis (CFA).

Although it does not assume you have read a previous book in this series on questionnaires (Ekinci, 2015), it would be advisable to do this if you are starting by constructing and administering your own questionnaire as this book is concerned with data analysis rather than collection. There will be some points in this book where I refer back to that text rather than explaining something fully again.

1.2 SURVEY DATA AND QUESTIONNAIRES

Surveys have long been used as an important method of data gathering in social science and other fields. As such, a wide range of methods have been developed over recent decades to enable the appropriate analysis of such data; in particular, in disciplines such as psychology this has become an important area of research in its own right (the field of *psychometrics* is devoted to studying the theory and technique of psychological measurement, which is predominantly survey-based).

One of the reasons surveys are so popular is their flexibility. Then can be used to collect both quantitative and qualitative data (this volume is concerned only with the quantitative part); they are sometimes the only valid way of collecting some quantitative data (e.g. opinions, attitudes, perceptions – things that cannot be measured directly); and they allow a large amount of data to be collected using consistent and relatively inexpensive methods.

Quantitative data within questionnaires can take on different forms, however – as it can with any source of data. Before going into detail on the types of methods that can be used, it is essential to understand these different data types.

The first distinction it is important to understand is that between *categorical* and *numerical* data. Categorical data refers to variables that can take on different categories – for example, sex, nationality and occupation. Each value represents a different thing, or category, but this is not a numerical quantity (although we may choose to use numbers as labels for these categories). Numerical data refers to variables that have a meaningful numerical value, whether on a naturally occurring or constructed scale – for example age, income, number of children, well-being measured on a scale from 1 to 10.

However, within these two major groups, there are sub-groups that it is important to understand: these are described and exemplified within Table 1.1.

Table 1.1   Six different types of questionnaire data

Major type	*Sub-type*	*Description*	*Examples*
Categorical	Nominal	Separate categories that have no natural ordering: just separate groups	Nationality (e.g. British, German, Chinese)
			Occupational group (e.g. teacher, doctor, lawyer)
	Binary	A special case of nominal data in which there are only two categories	Sex*
			Questions requiring a 'Yes/No' response
	Ordinal	Separate categories that have a natural and consistent ordering – so it is always possible to say whether one category is higher than another	Job grade (e.g. grades 1, 2, 3, 4, 5)
			Class of degree awarded (e.g. First, Upper second, Lower second, third)
Numerical	Continuous: interval	A number representing a quantity, but can be measured on any scale, not necessarily a naturally occurring one (and therefore the value 0 usually has no natural interpretation as it would for a ratio variable)	Job satisfaction (measured on a scale from 1-7)
			Temperature (if measured in °Celsius or °Fahrenheit – if measured in Kelvin this would be a ratio variable)

Major type	Sub-type	Description	Examples
	Continuous: ratio	A number, which theoretically can take on any possible value within a given range, and measured on a consistent scale such that the value 0 represents an absence of the quality being observed. The accuracy of the number is constrained only by the measurement available	Age Height
	Discrete	Often referred to as a 'count' variable, this is usually a count score that can take on only whole numbers. It is most commonly used when the count is generally low: if the count is very high (e.g. population of countries) then it would usually be treated as a continuous (ratio) variable instead	Number of previous jobs Number of children

*Of course this is not necessarily a simple binary variable as it fails to take into account transgender people – however, it is often measured in a binary way.

The distinction between these different types and sub-types is crucial for making decisions about analysis. Some types of analysis (e.g. correlations) only make sense with continuous data; some (e.g. chi-squared tests) only make sense with categorical data; some (e.g. one-way ANOVA) require a mixture of the two. However, these types of analysis are covered in Scherbaum and Shockley (2015), and will only be mentioned briefly in this book.

For the majority of this book we will concern ourselves with one particular type of data that is very common in questionnaires, but doesn't fit neatly into the categorization in Table 1.1: Likert scales.

1.3 LIKERT SCALES

Likert scales, named after the twentieth-century American psychologist Rensis Likert, are a method of measuring a variable (construct) that cannot be directly measured, by asking respondents to what extent they agree with a series of statements. Each statement is known as an 'item'; technically, a Likert scale is the summation (or average) of the different items, although it is sometimes used to refer to an individual item as well.

For example, a set of three items relating to extraversion (Lang et al., 2011) is:

- I see myself as someone who is talkative.
- I see myself as someone who is outgoing, sociable.
- I see myself as someone who is reserved.

For each item, the respondent would typically choose from one of the following options:

- Strongly disagree.
- Disagree.
- Neither agree nor disagree.
- Agree.
- Strongly agree.

Sometimes a different set of response categories might be used: for example, options ranging from 'Very dissatisfied' to 'Very satisfied', or from 'Not at all' to 'All the time'. Technically these should be referred to as Likert-type scales, as the original definition of Likert scales refers to items asking about the level of agreement only; however, it is common for all such scales to be referred to as Likert scales, and so this book will use the term 'Likert scales' to refer to all sets of items with such rating scales.

The number of response options may vary: in the above example there were five, but this may be four, six, seven or indeed any higher number. Note that if there are an odd number of items, then a symmetrical scale will yield a neutral or average item (e.g. 'Neither agree nor disagree') whereas an even number of items (e.g. six) will not.

In any case, each item should be considered as an *ordinal* variable. That is, the respondent chooses from one of a number of ordered categories. However, when taken together this changes. The purpose of asking three separate questions about extraversion here is not that the individual items are themselves of particular interest, but that between them they should give a better overall indication of the level of extraversion. Therefore a single score for the construct (extraversion) needs to be created.

For this purpose, a number is assigned to each of the responses – typically these would be 1, 2, 3, 4, 5 for the above example, although for the third question (which measures the extent to which someone is reserved – the opposite of what we would

1. To what extent do you agree with the following?	Strongly disagree (1)	Disagree (2)	Neither agree nor disagree (3)	Agree (4)	Strongly agree (5)
a. I see myself as someone who is talkative	☐	☐	☐	☐	☐
b. I see myself as someone who is outgoing, sociable	☐	☐	☐	☐	☐
c. I see myself as someone who is reserved	☐	☐	☐	☐	☐

Figure 1.1 Lang et al.'s (2011) extraversion scale in questionnaire form

expect for an extravert) a response of 'strongly disagree' means higher extraversion, and therefore we would code these responses as 5, 4, 3, 2, 1 respectively. This is often referred to as a 'negatively worded question'.[1]

The overall score for extraversion, then, would be calculated as the average – the arithmetic mean – or, alternatively, the sum of these three item scores. So, for example, if someone responded 'Strongly agree' to 'I see myself as someone who is talkative' this would be scored 5; if they responded 'Neither agree nor disagree' to 'I see myself as someone who is outgoing, sociable' this would be scored 3; and if they responded 'Disagree' to 'I see myself as someone who is reserved', this would be scored 4 (because it is a negatively worded question). The overall extraversion score for this individual, then, would be $(5 + 3 + 4) \div 3 = 4.0$.

You may notice that, by doing this, we are treating the ordinal measurement of the individual items in a more numerical way, and the eventual score for extraversion is no longer categorical, but actually resembles an interval variable. In fact, it is then usually treated in analysis as if it is a continuous, numerical variable.

Is this justified? Research suggests that it can be, but only if the Likert scale (or just 'scale') has good reliability and validity – concepts that are hugely important in survey research, and will be the focus for large sections of this book. These will be introduced formally in Chapter 2.

1.4 CLASSICAL TEST THEORY

Classical test theory (CTT) is the measurement theory that underlies the techniques being described in this book. It was developed by Mel Novick, who first published the codification in 1966 (Novick, 1966). It is based around the idea that any measured score consists of two parts – a *true* score and an *error*. The 'error' may represent measurement error, and other types of random or systematic error too – examples of these will be shown in the next chapter. As we will also see in Chapter 2, this can be expressed in a formal mathematical way that allows us to express concepts like reliability and validity in a more formal way.

A key concept in CTT is that, even though our measurement may be constrained by the tools we used, the underlying (true) score is on a continuum. Thus, when someone answers a question such as 'I see myself as someone who is talkative', their true perception of how talkative they are could fall anywhere within a given range – between the point where they would only answer 'strongly disagree' and the point where they would answer 'strongly agree'. If they consider themselves to be quite talkative, for instance, but perhaps not as much as some other people they know, then their true perception may fall somewhere between the points represented by 'agree' and

---

[1] In practice, we would normally start by coding everything as 1, 2, 3, 4, 5, and then recoding any negatively scored items later using computer software – see Chapter 3.

e' – it would be up to the respondent to choose which the more appro-
~s. Thus the item, which appears as an ordinal measurement, actually
ınt measurement of a continuous underlying measure.

1.5 TYPES OF ANALYSIS USING SURVEY DATA

When it comes to data analysis, there will normally be several possible stages. Which stages you use, and which types of analysis you apply at each stage, depend on the research questions and objectives, and the types of data available to you. As each type of analysis has its own type of output and possible conclusions, it is highly important that the correct methods of analysis are selected. This is why it is important to consider the type of analysis to be done, and therefore the types of data required, before data are even col-lected. However, sometimes this is not possible – for example, if using secondary data – so the procedures described in this book allow for the possibility of non-ideal situations also.

1.5.1 Stage 1 – data tidying

This stage does not (usually) lead to conclusions relating to the research objectives themselves, but is an essential first step before undertaking the other stages. After data entry, there will often be a number of tasks needing to be performed on a data set before it is ready to be analysed fully. Some of these are routine with any data set – for example, checking for ineligible values, noting missing data – but others are particularly useful with scale data from surveys.

   Where data from multi-item scales have been collected, one aim of this stage is to get an overall score for each scale (e.g. a score for 'extraversion' in the example in section 1.3 above). However, before this can be calculated the following steps should be performed:

- Any negatively worded items should be *recoded*, so that all items have the same 'valence' (that is, a high score either consistently represents a high amount of the quality being measured, or consistently represents a low amount).
- The scale *reliability* should be checked.
- Sometimes (although not always) the scale *validity* should be checked by using fac-tor analysis (either exploratory or confirmatory).
- If the reliability and validity are sufficient, then an overall scale score can be calcu-lated as the average score across the items.

1.5.2 Stage 2 – descriptive analysis

Descriptive analysis is about saying what is in your data set – sometimes this is a sample from a larger population; other times, it might represent the complete set of data available for a given topic. Either way, there are different sets of procedures available for different purposes.

For any numerical data, there are a range of different statistics available that can describe each variable – the mean and median are often used to describe the average, or central, value of a variable; the standard deviation and interquartile range are among several statistics used to describe the spread of a variable; and more advanced statistics such as skewness and kurtosis describe the shape of a variable's distribution.

For categorical data, frequencies and percentages in each category usually suffice, although if there are a large number of categories these might sometimes be grouped into broader categories first.

In either case, graphs can be used for helping to display this information: histograms for numerical variables (although bar charts may be preferred for discrete variables with relatively few values), and either bar charts or pie charts for categorical variables.

The descriptive analysis will often also include comparison of different variables, particularly if this is one of the research objectives. For example, if two categorical variables are to be compared, this is often best achieved by a cross-tabulation; if there are relatively few categories then a clustered bar chart may also be helpful.

If a categorical variable and a numerical variable are to be compared, then descriptive statistics of the numerical variable for each category of the categorical value are a useful way to display this. Various types of graph (e.g. bar charts, boxplots) can also help display this graphically.

To compare two numerical variables, a correlation is often used, accompanied by a scatter plot. More complex techniques may aim to summarize multiple variables at once, for example cluster analysis or principal components analysis (PCA).

This list of methods is not exhaustive, but gives some examples of the most typical procedures used.

1.5.3 Stage 3 – inferential analysis

Very often the data available represent a sample from a wider population (whether that is a population of organizations, or employees, or specific types of customer, or all people, or whatever); the research questions are not really so much about the sample as about the population, and so inferential analysis is used to draw inferences from the sample about the wider population.

In this type of analysis, the sample is usually chosen to be broadly representative of the whole population – for example, if wanting to learn about customers of a business, it might involve a completely random selection of people from a customer database (a 'simple random sample'), a random selection from within each of several types of customer (e.g. one-off customers, occasional customers, regular customers – this would be a 'stratified random sample'), or various other methods. The size of the sample can be quite small compared with the whole population, however, and still yield fairly accurate estimates for the whole population: for example, a sample of 100 will often yield quite good results, and a sample of 1,000 can give very accurate results indeed – even if the population size is in the millions.

This does depend on appropriate methods of analysis being used, however. A whole range of different techniques might be used here, depending on what the aim of the analysis is, and how many variables are involved:

- If a single variable is involved (e.g. estimating what proportion of a population is likely to vote for a particular candidate in a forthcoming election), then descriptive methods combined with confidence intervals are most likely to be used.
- If comparing two variables, then relatively simple techniques such as t-tests, one-way ANOVA, chi-squared tests and correlations can be employed.
- If more than two variables are involved, then more complex methods such as multiple regression, multi-way ANOVA, log-linear modelling and generalized linear models may be used.

For more on the types of analysis used in stages 2 and 3, see the volume in this series (Scherbaum and Shockley, 2015), which covers these in detail.

1.6 THE REMAINDER OF THIS BOOK

The majority of this book is concerned with the survey-specific parts of stage 1 analysis, as covered in section 1.5.1.

Chapter 2 will discuss the foundations of classical test theory, and the epistemological and methodological assumptions that underpin it. Chapter 3 will summarize the procedures used, describing the process of research from the end of data collection to the end of the analysis covered in this volume. The details of how to conduct these methods of analysis will be shown in Chapter 4, with some examples from the management literature shown in Chapter 5. Finally, Chapter 6 will examine some of the strengths and weaknesses of the methods, as well as discussing some of the more contentious decision-making criteria.

1.7 CHAPTER SUMMARY

In this chapter we have introduced quantitative survey data, classical test theory and an outline of the process for conducting analysis with this data. This chapter was not intended to give sufficient detail about these matters, but to serve as an introduction to the topic. These will now be expanded upon in subsequent chapters.

CHAPTER REFERENCES

Ekinci, Y. (2015) *Designing Research Questionnaires for Business and Management Students*. London: Sage.

Lang, F.R., John, D., Lüdtke, O., Schupp, J. and Wagner, G.G. (2011) Short assessment of the Big Five: robust across survey methods except telephone interviewing. *Behavioral Research Methods*, 43(2), 548–567.

Novick, M.R. (1966) The axioms and principal results of classical test theory. *Journal of Mathematical Psychology*, 3, 1–18.

Scherbaum, C. and Shockley, K. (2015) *Analysing Quantitative Data for Business and Management Students*. London: Sage.

2

METHODOLOGICAL ASSUMPTIONS, RELIABILITY AND VALIDITY

2.1 CHAPTER OVERVIEW

This chapter introduces some of the ideas and assumptions underlying the measurement and analysis of quantitative survey data - particularly focusing on the assumptions of classical test theory, and the concepts of reliability and validity. It should give a solid basis for understanding the detail of the analysis techniques described in the rest of the book. We begin by looking at the philosophical underpinnings of quantitative survey data in general and classical test theory in particular, and then study the important areas of reliability and validity in more detail.

2.2 ONTOLOGY AND EPISTEMOLOGY

Quantitative methods are often associated with the positivist philosophy, although this is not exclusively the case. According to positivism, there is an objective reality, and measurement tools are used to convert that reality into variables. With much quantitative research, particularly in the natural sciences, this approach fits well.

However, for questionnaire surveys, it is easy to see why that might not be the case. In the alternative perspective of interpretivism, the focus is on understanding the differences between the perceptions of participants, often portrayed in their role as 'social actors' - different participants will construct their own view of reality, and it is these views that are important rather than attempting to measure an objective reality (which may or may not exist).

Interpretivist approaches are often used in qualitative research; however, due to the individual nature of questionnaire responses - how an individual responds to a question depends on their understanding and interpretation of the meaning of that question – it is equally possible that an interpretivist study might make use of questionnaire data. However, there is still by necessity an assumption that the measurement tools (questions) are attempting to measure some underlying construct – but that the underlying construct is a perception, rather than a reality. This can obviously affect the interpretation of the findings.

Likewise, quantitative methods are more often associated with deductive, rather than inductive, research. Deductive research – the testing of theory that exists before data are collected – certainly fits clearly with the inferential statistics approach. However, if a more descriptive approach is taken, then this can be used in an inductive way – i.e. to generate and develop theory from data. Even if more complex analyses are conducted, if these are done using an exploratory approach (rather than testing hypotheses), then this would qualify as inductive research. Of course, using a questionnaire survey can lend itself to both approaches, and some studies may use a mixture.

2.3 RELIABILITY AND VALIDITY

Reliability and validity are separate but complementary ideas describing how useful a measurement tool is (in this context, the question(s) under consideration are the 'tool'). Understanding the meaning of these terms is critical in being able to assess how good a questionnaire is – in particular multi-item scales.

In broad terms, reliability is defined as the extent to which a measurement is free from error – or to put it another way, how consistent the measurement would be if it were repeated. Validity is defined as the extent to which a tool measures what it is supposed to be measuring (in other words, whether on average it would measure the correct thing, even if there may be error with individual measurements).

It may be easiest to understand this by considering a non-questionnaire example. Let's imagine that a researcher's true weight is 65kg. She uses a set of weighing scales to measure this – these are her measurement tool.

If the researcher weighs herself four times in quick succession, it would be hoped that the reading would be the same each time. If this is the case, then the scales would be *reliable* – because there is no error associated with each individual measurement. However, if the weight given was something other than 65kg, then the scales would not be valid – as they are not measuring the weight correctly.

Consider these four scenarios:

1. The four readings (in kg) are 65, 65, 65, 65. In this case the tool would be both reliable and valid.
2. The four readings are 62, 64, 66, 68. This would not be reliable, as each measurement is subject to some error (a lot of error in two cases). However, the average (mean) weight is correct, so the tool may still be valid.

3. The four readings are 68, 68, 68, 68. In this case the tool appears reliable, as the readings are consistent. However, it is certainly not valid, as the consistent reading is different from the true value.
4. The four readings are 66, 68, 70, 72. In this case the tool would be neither reliable nor valid (as the mean is well above 65).

You may already have spotted a problem with determining these concepts. Reliability is relatively easy to determine, because by examining repeated measurements it can be seen whether there is the consistency required. Within questionnaires we do not usually ask the same questions several times – but instead we often ask closely related questions, forming part of a multi-item scale. As will be seen later in this chapter, this allows us to calculate a form of reliability that is commonly understood.

However, it is more difficult to determine validity. In scenario 3 above, the four readings are identical, and if we were to know no better, we may assume that because the tool is reliable, we can trust the reading it gives us. However, in this case we know that the reading is incorrect; normally, however, we cannot know this. If the researcher already knew that her correct weight was 65kg, then she would have no need to measure it!

Therefore it takes a lot more effort to assess validity. There are various ways of doing this – these will be described later in the chapter, and in later chapters – but the methods are not generally possible without other data. Within a questionnaire, for example, we may ask the three questions introduced in Chapter 1 about extraversion, but how do we know that these are really measuring extraversion, as opposed to a different (but related) concept such as positivity? To know this requires a series of tests comparing the three-item scale we are considering with other scales that measure similar and different measures. This requires a lot of data and a lot of hard work – this is one reason why, wherever possible, it is better to use questionnaire scales for which evidence of validity has already been published.

Later in this chapter more formal definitions of reliability and validity, as relate to questionnaire multi-item scales, will be introduced. However, this first requires a formal definition of classical test theory.

2.4 CLASSICAL TEST THEORY

Classical test theory (CTT), formally codified by Novick (1966), is the theory underlying questionnaire scale measurement. The basic idea is that there is a true score – a value that we are trying to measure, which may be an objective or subjective value – and that our measurement of this consists of two parts: the true score plus some error.

Although this book will be relatively light on algebra and mathematics, there are some concepts that can be most easily expressed in algebraic form. Thus, according to CTT, a measurement x_i comprises a true score t_i and an error e_i:

$$x_i = t_i + e_i$$

The true score is, of course, usually unknown (otherwise there would be no need to do the measurement in this way); therefore, the amount of error is generally uncertain also.

A crucial assumption of CTT is that the error is independent of the true score - that is, a low score is just as likely to contain error as a high score, and this error could be positive or negative. This may or may not stand up to closer scrutiny; however, very often it is at least close enough to being true (i.e. any dependence is a small part of the error) that we can effectively ignore any violation of this assumption.

Moreover, the error could take on various different forms, as shown in the examples in Box 2.1.

Box 2.1   Examples of different forms of measurement error

Example 1

An individual is asked how long he has worked in his organization. The actual answer is nine years, but unable to recall this information accurately when completing the questionnaire, he answers with an estimate of ten years.

In this case the measured score (x_i) is 10 years, the true score (t_i) is 9 years, meaning that the error (e_i) is 1 year. This error is best described as random error as there is no systematic reason for the estimate to be incorrect - it is purely down to the individual's recall ability.

Example 2

A respondent is asked to rate her job performance on a scale from 1 to 5, where 1 represents the worst imaginable performance, and 5 the best imaginable performance. If she were to consider this carefully, her perception of her actual performance might be 3.7 (i.e. two thirds of the way up the scale). However, the options available are 1, 2, 3, 4 and 5, so she answers with a 4.

Here, the measured score (x_i) is 4, but the true score (t_i) is 3.7, meaning that the error (e_i) is 0.3. This would be called method error because the error is forced upon the score by the blunt nature of the tool - only whole numbers can be chosen. Therefore, for a true score of 3.7, this is the minimum possible error that can be found.

Example 3

A customer is asked to rate his satisfaction with a product on a scale from 1 to 7. His average satisfaction level with this product would actually be around 5.1, but he is in a good mood when completing the questionnaire, and so gives a rating of 6.

Here, the measured score (x_i) is 6, but the true score (t_i) is 5.1, meaning that the error (e_i) is 0.9. This would be called method bias because the score is biased upwards not by chance, and not by any particular limitation with the response scale (he could have chosen 5, and been a lot closer), but because the nature of his response was influenced by an outside characteristic – his mood. This is dangerous because the same thing could influence other responses on the same questionnaire, which could result in inflated correlations between scores. This is known as common method bias, and is very difficult to avoid when only using questionnaire data.

In reality, we don't know which of these (or other) sources of error may be contributing to the measured score. It is likely that many scores will have multiple sources of error: sometimes these might cancel each other out, other times they may even exacerbate each other. However, often they will just be separate and independent sources of error, contributing to the overall measurement error (e_i).

Therefore the aim of good measurement is to limit the amount of error as far as possible – that is, to have as high reliability as possible.

2.5 RELIABILITY WITHIN CLASSICAL TEST THEORY

We have already established that reliability is defined as the extent to which a measurement is free from error. There is a more formal definition, however: the proportion of variance in a measurement that is due to differences in the true score, as opposed to error.

Within CTT, we have seen that the measured score comprises the true score and an error:

$$x_i = t_i + e_i$$

We have also seen that the error is assumed to be independent of the true score. This independence means that the variance in the measured score can be decomposed in a straightforward way:

$$\sigma_x = \sigma_t + \sigma_e$$

where σ_x, σ_t and σ_e are the variances of x_i, t_i and e_i respectively. That is, the variance of the measured score is equal to the sum of the variance in the true score and the error variance. It follows that reliability can be defined as:

$$\rho = \sigma_t/\sigma_x = \sigma_t/(\sigma_x + \sigma_e)$$

However, even this does not tell us how it should be calculated as we do not know what σ_x, σ_t and σ_e are: therefore we have to estimate these.

There are two common ways of estimating reliability with questionnaire data: one that can work with any numerical data, and one that works specifically for multi-item scales. Analogous to the example given earlier, about weighing oneself repeatedly, the first method is called *test-retest reliability*. As the name suggests, it relies on performing a test (questionnaire measure) once, and then doing it again, and comparing the results. The measure of reliability then is simply the (Pearson) correlation between the two measurements.[1] However, this relies on certain assumptions:

- The participants are the same in both surveys.
- The survey questions are identical – not just those being tested, but any others in the questionnaire as well in case these influence the responses to the measure under scrutiny.
- The conditions under which the questionnaire is answered are identical.
- The time between the survey administrations is relatively short.
- There have been no changes that might affect the variable being studied.

This, therefore, is relatively unusual: it would not be common to conduct the same survey on the same participants twice in quick succession. Sometimes this might be done with the aim of evaluating some type of intervention – but this would then violate the final assumption. Realistically this is most likely to be done as part of a scale development process, when the benefits of assessing test-retest reliability can be worth the extra effort required.

For multi-item scales, however, a short-cut is possible. This is because of the assumption, under CTT, that each of the items is an indicator of the overall variable – the underlying construct, such as extraversion in the previous example. Therefore the different items used in this measure are, in one sense, repeated measurements of the same thing. They are not identical, and therefore we wouldn't necessarily expect the responses to be identical – but we would certainly expect them to be close (on average). We can measure this using a different type of reliability: *internal consistency* (so called because the different items within a scale are expected to be fairly consistent with each other).

Internal consistency is most commonly measured using an index known as coefficient alpha, or Cronbach's alpha (after the American psychologist Lee Cronbach,

---

[1] Some authors suggest using a different type of correlation – the *intraclass* correlation (ICC). This takes into account the variation within individual respondents as well, comparing it with the variation between respondents, whereas the Pearson correlation (an *interclass* correlation) compares only the patterns of responses between the two surveys. For example, the correlation between two scores can be 1 if the scores themselves are different, but the pattern of the scores is identical (e.g. adding 1.0 to each score). However, for an ICC to be 1, the scores would need to be identical.

who developed it in 1951). It has slightly different versions, but is normally used in its standardized form, which has the following formula:

$$\alpha = \frac{k\bar{r}}{1 + (k-1)\bar{r}}$$

where k is the number of items, and $\bar{r}$ is the mean inter-item correlation. If this value is above 0.8 it is considered adequate, although some authors have claimed that values of 0.7 or higher are acceptable too (see Chapter 6 for more on this issue).

Many statistical software programmes, such as SPSS, will calculate Cronbach's alpha easily, and will provide helpful evaluation tools such as displaying what Cronbach's alpha would be if an item were to be removed from the scale – which can be helpful if the reliability is too low, or if you are deciding between options for a new scale. This procedure will be discussed in detail in Chapter 4.

Box 2.2   Other types of reliability

Because 'reliability' is defined as the extent to which a tool is free from measurement error, it can be considered in different ways. This is partly because of the multiple possible sources of error, and also partly because the amount of error cannot be determined exactly, but must be estimated based on certain assumptions. The principal assumption underlying test–retest reliability is that a test's lack of accuracy is due to random error that will change from time to time. The principal assumption underlying internal consistency is that a test's lack of accuracy is due to different elements (or items) of the measurement being more or less similar to the underlying construct being measured. Either or both of these things might be true. However, there are other ways of measuring reliability in different circumstances.

Split-half reliability is another way of capturing the reliability of a multi-item scale. It relies on the administration of the whole scale to a sample, and then splitting the scale into two halves (often at random), and then correlating the two halves with each other. If the two halves correlate very strongly, then this suggests they are almost equally good at estimating the construct being measured, and therefore (a) the overall scale will be an even better measure, and (b) a shorter scale may suffice. However, this would only really work in the case of a long scale (one with many items) – if a scale is relatively short to begin with (say, six items or fewer) then the split-half reliability is unlikely to be high due to the possible extent of random variation within each item. As such, split-half reliability is rarely used in practice.

(Continued)

(Continued)

Similarly, *parallel-forms reliability* involves taking two different versions of the same test (formed with the same content and question type). If both forms yield similar results (i.e. the two tests have high correlations), then it suggests that both are reliable.

Inter-rater reliability is a useful tool when an assessment of measurement is made by different people. It is based on the assumption that measurement error may be down to the individual making the assessment – for example, if customers are rating a shop's level of service, they will all have had slightly different experiences. It is generally measured using a form of intraclass correlation (ICC), which compares the amount of variation between raters (the people making the measurements, i.e. the customers in this example) with the amount of variation between targets (the things they are rating, i.e. shops in this example). For a full discussion of interclass correlations see Shrout and Fleiss (1979).

2.7 DIFFERENT TYPES OF VALIDITY

As a reminder, the validity of a test is the extent to which it measures what it is supposed to measure. This is sometimes referred to as the *construct validity* (to distinguish it from other types of validity – e.g. internal and external validity, which refer to how well conclusions can be drawn from a study).

However, even within the definition of construct validity there are several different aspects to consider. Broadly, these fit into three areas:

- Content and face validity – these reflect the extent to which a measurement matches its definition. Content validity is about whether all aspects of a definition are covered; face validity is about whether it 'looks' right (e.g. whether an expert would look at the three questions described in Chapter 1 measuring extraversion, and conclude that it is a measure of extraversion as opposed to a different construct, such as enthusiasm). Neither content nor face validity can be quantified easily, so this is usually assessed via expert opinion.
- Criterion-related validity – this is the extent to which a measure is similar to other variables to which it is expected to be similar (this is usually determined based on theory). This is sometimes called concurrent or convergent validity, and it includes the concept of 'predictive validity' – that is, whether a measurement predicts a future measurement of something else, e.g. whether a measurement of job satisfaction predicts job performance. It is usually assessed using relatively simple statistical tests such as correlation and regression.

- Discriminant validity – this is the extent to which a measure can be distinguished from other measures that are related, but different. For example, is a measure of job satisfaction sufficiently different from measures of organizational commitment and life satisfaction that it can be said to be a truly different construct? Unless this is established, then it is difficult to claim that something distinctive is being measured. Discriminant validity (sometimes known as divergent validity) is usually assessed with more sophisticated statistical methods such as exploratory and confirmatory factor analysis.

In Chapter 3 we will see suggestions about how you should go about examining validity on your own data, depending on how well established the measurements are. Chapter 4 will include guidance on how to conduct the statistical analyses.

2.7 MULTI-ITEM SCALES

We have already seen an example of a multi-item scale: in Chapter 1, the three-item scale for measuring extraversion was a fairly typical example of such a measure (although often scales will include many more than three items). Such scales are commonplace in questionnaire research, because they can have far superior measurement properties. This is for several reasons:

- They tend to have superior reliability. This manifests itself in two ways: first, the use of a single item would only leave a small number of possible values, representing the different response options (often between 4 and 7). In reality, however, it will often be used to measure an underlying construct that is continuous in nature. Therefore the coarseness of the response scale often leads to some measurement error (as one example in section 2.4 demonstrates).
- The other reason reliability is higher with multi-item scales is because there is often some internal consistency among the items, and this tends to increase as more items are included. The formula for Cronbach's alpha (shown in section 2.5) indicates why this happens: as the number of items, k, increases, then so does the reliability – even when the mean inter-item correlation remains the same. For example, an eight-item measure with reliability of 0.90 would have a reliability of 0.82 if only four items (with the same properties) were included.
- Multi-item scales are often more valid measures of constructs that cannot be measured directly. This is demonstrated with the example from Chapter 1 of the three-item scale measuring extraversion. It is commonly agreed that it is not possible to judge someone's extraversion accurately by asking a single question (and thus a single item would not have good face validity); however, by covering different aspects of the construct of extraversion (talkative, outgoing, sociable, not reserved), the items ensure that the measure has good content validity.

- Finally, it is far easier to establish discriminant validity - i.e. that the tool is measuring something different from other tools - when multi-item scales are used. This is because the statistical techniques that are used to establish this (exploratory factor analysis, confirmatory factor analysis) do not work well (if at all) when single-item measures are used.

Overall, the advantages of multi-item scales are significant when it comes to the quality of measurement of many variables. The principal disadvantage is that it requires more questions to be asked; however, if the quality of measurement is important (as it should be in research), then this is usually a price worth paying. Scales for your research should be selected based on published evidence of reliability and validity. Only if no appropriate scale exists already should a new one be developed - as the process of establishing reliability and validity is long, hard and expensive.

   Much of the rest of this book will deal with multi-item scales as the main method of measurement. In Chapter 3 we will discuss different possible approaches for using and analysing such measures, before these are demonstrated in Chapter 4.

2.8 CHAPTER SUMMARY

In this chapter we have considered the philosophical underpinnings of quantitative survey data in general and classical test theory in particular, examining what the assumptions are, and what this means in terms of the measurement of constructs via questionnaires. We have then investigated the concepts of reliability and validity in more depth, particularly with reference to classical test theory: describing the different sources of measurement error that cause lack of reliability, different forms of reliability and different forms of validity. The chapter finished by looking at multi-item scales, which are one of the most common forms of quantitative data collection in surveys. The analysis of such scales will be covered in detail in the rest of this book.

CHAPTER REFERENCES

Cronbach, L.J. (1951) Coefficient alpha and the internal structure of tests. *Psychometrika*, 16, 297-334.

Novick, M.R. (1966) The axioms and principal results of classical test theory. *Journal of Mathematical Psychology*, 3, 1-18.

Shrout, P.E. and Fleiss, J.L. (1979) Intraclass correlations: uses in assessing rater reliability. *Psychological Bulletin*, 86(2), 420.

3

BASIC COMPONENTS OF ANALYSING
QUANTITATIVE SURVEY DATA

3.1 CHAPTER OVERVIEW

In this chapter we illustrate the sequence of steps you would undertake, and decisions you will need to make, once you have collected your survey data, in particular data from multi-item scales. How to carry out the procedures themselves will be covered in Chapter 4.

We'll start by assuming you have used a survey to collect data, and now want to begin analysis. If you have collected variables that are already in exactly the correct form for analysis, then this is straightforward: you can enter the data directly from the questionnaires into appropriate statistical software (e.g. SPSS) and conduct the analysis that you have planned; this is likely to involve some descriptive analysis and possibly some hypothesis testing or other specific analysis (some of these methods are mentioned in section 3.5).

However, if you are using multi-item scales (sets of questions that are designed to measure a single construct or variable) for some or all of your variables, there are a number of steps you should go through first, as indicated in Figure 3.1. These are then described in the remaining sections of this chapter.

3.2 SETTING UP SURVEY DATA FOR ANALYSIS: DATA ENTRY AND CLEANING

In the first place, data need to be entered into an appropriate software program. This should be chosen with a view to what subsequent analysis is needed. So, for example, Microsoft Excel is a commonly used program for data storage and some types of

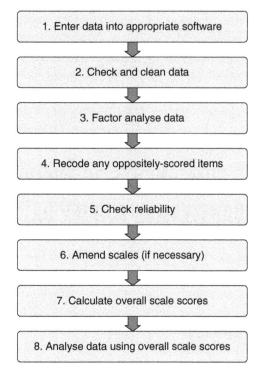

Figure 3.1 Steps for preparing and analysing multi-item scale data

analysis; however, it does not contain built-in procedures (or 'functions') for some of the required stages here, such as factor analysis and reliability analysis. Therefore it would be advisable to use a more specialist software package, such as SPSS, Stata or SAS. The examples in this book use SPSS, which is probably the most commonly used statistical software for management and social science students.

In the first instance, there should be one column (or variable) per item (usually a question) in the questionnaire. For each item, a code number should be assigned to each possible response. Typically these would be 1 for the first response listed, with increasing numbers for each other response – so if the possible responses were 'Strongly disagree', 'Disagree', 'Neutral', 'Agree' and 'Strongly agree', these would be coded as 1, 2, 3, 4 and 5 respectively. Each row represents a different respondent, and so the data may look similar to that in Figure 3.2.

However, it is important that any other relevant information is included within the data file: so for example in SPSS, variable labels and value labels should be added for each variable. This allows you to interpret what each number in the data file means: for example, the 4 in the first row of column Q1.1 (in Figure 3.2) would mean that that particular item (the text of which would be given in the variable label, shown in the Variable View) had a response of 'Agree' from the respondent with ID number 1.

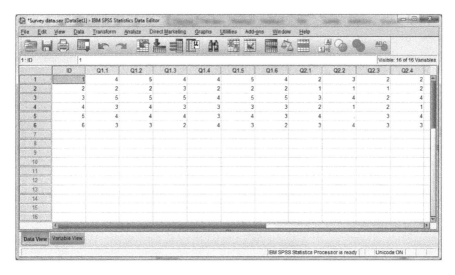

Figure 3.2 An example of questionnaire data being entered into SPSS

Reprint Courtesy of International Business Machines Corporation, © International Business Machines Corporation

Box 3.1   A tip about entering survey data

Before entering or transferring data, it is a good idea to take a blank copy of the questionnaire, and write on the variable names you plan to use, as well as the codes you will use for the responses (see Figure 3.3). This will help ensure consistency and can be a useful reference guide when entering data (and beyond).

1. About you

Age: AGE —————— (yrs)	Are you? SEX Male ☐ 1 Female ☐ 2
Occupational group: OCCGROUP Medical/dental ☐ 1 Nursing/midwifery ☐ 2 Senior managers ☐ 3	Allied Health Professional ☐ 4 Administrative/clerical ☐ 5 Ancillary ☐ 6

(Continued)

(Continued)

2. To what extent do you agree with the following?	Strongly disagree	Disagree	Neither agree nor disagree	Agree	Strongly agree
FEED 1 a. I receive clear feedback on my work performance from my manager/supervisor	☐	☐	☐	☐	☐
FEED 2 b. Usually know whether or not my work is satisfactory on this job	☐	☐	☐	☐	☐
FEED 3 c. I often have trouble figuring out whether I am doing well or poorly on this job	☐ *1*	☐ *2*	☐ *3*	☐ *4*	☐ *5*

Figure 3.3

Sometimes data may be read in from other software: for example, if an online survey programme such as SurveyMonkey or Qualtrics is used, it may create an Excel data file (or even an SPSS one). This removes the hassle of entering the data manually, although care should still be taken to ensure the data are set up exactly as described above. This may require appropriate renaming of variables, inserting of variable names and coding of value labels (as well as sometimes recoding of the values themselves).

Box 3.2   A tip about naming variables

If you have several items as part of a question block, or known to be part of the same multi-item scale, it may be advisable to give them similar variable names, but with sequentially numbered endings: for example, in the data in Figure 3.2, the first six items form a scale and are named Q1.1, Q1.2, Q1.3, Q1.4, Q1.5 and Q1.6. If you know that the scale is supposed to represent a certain construct, say job performance, then you might name them accordingly – e.g. jobperf1, jobperf 2, etc.

I find that the most straightforward way to enter scale data is so that the first response listed is coded as 1, the second response coded as 2, and so on. In many cases, this also reflects the scoring of the variables that you will want to use. Sometimes, however, individual items are 'reverse-scored': in other words, a more positive answer (e.g. agreeing with a negatively worded statement) actually represents the opposite effect of the majority of items (e.g. where statements are worded positively). For example, in the extraversion scale described in section 1.3, the third item is 'I see myself as someone who is reserved'. Agreement with this would imply the respondent was less extravert (and more introvert), whereas agreement on the other items in the scale would imply the respondent was more extravert.

In such cases, it is generally easier to recode the reverse-scored item, so that rather than 'Strongly disagree' and 'Strongly agree' being coded as 1 and 5 respectively, they would actually be coded as 5 and 1 respectively (so that a high score is associated with more extravert people for all the items). Although this can be done directly while entering the data, it can lead to data entry being more complex, taking longer and being more prone to mistakes. Rather, it is easier if all values are entered in the order they appear in the questionnaire, and then reverse-scored items can be recoded later. This can be accomplished easily using SPSS.

Box 3.3   SPSS example – recoding variables

SPSS makes recoding variables a relatively simple procedure. There are two options available: recoding into the same variables (which overwrites the previous values), and recoding into different variables (which enables you to create new variables). The latter method is preferable in most circumstances, so that the original version of the variable (and the original data) is kept as well (particularly important if the recoding involves collapsing multiple values into a single new category).

Let's say we want to reverse-code the third item in the extraversion scale, which we have given variable name 'extra3'. In SPSS we would first go to the 'Transform' menu and choose 'Recode into different variables'. We then need to select the variable we will be recoding (extra3), and choose a name and label for the recoded version of the variable. A recommended name would be extra3r – representing the variable extra3, with an 'r' on the end to show it is recoded. Note that you need to click 'Change' before this naming/labelling is finalized.

The important part of this procedure, though, is specifying what values of the variable are changed to what. To achieve this, you first need to click 'Old and New Values'. This opens up another box in which you state the values of the original variable (on the left-hand side), and what values they become in the new variable (on the right-hand side). For Likert scale items this can be done just using the uppermost 'Value' boxes on each side. Take care to enter each of the possible values of the original variable in turn (don't miss any out, even those that are staying the same),

(Continued)

(Continued)

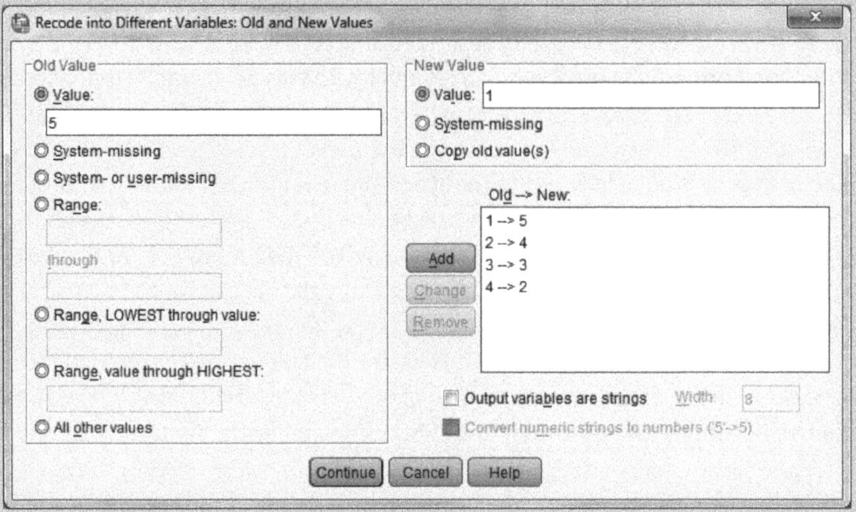

Figure 3.4

Reprint Courtesy of International Business Machines Corporation, © International Business Machines Corporation

and after specifying each pair of old value and new value, click 'Add' to ensure they register. For a response scale with options 1 to 5, this would mean the old value 1 becomes new value 5, 2 becomes 4, 3 becomes 3, 4 becomes 2, and 5 becomes 1.

To complete the procedure, you would click 'Continue' and then 'OK'. It would be advisable at this point to go to the Variable View, add correct value labels for the new variable, and make any other necessary amendments before saving the data file.

Note that this can also be accomplished using SPSS syntax, with the following commands:

recode extra3 (1 = 5)(2 = 4)(3 = 3)(4 = 2)(5 = 1) into extra3r.

execute.

With the syntax version, multiple variables can be recoded at once – this can save a lot of time if there are several items that need exactly the same recoding.

Sometimes the need to recode items is not obvious at first: it may become apparent at later stages, e.g. after conducting factor analysis. If so, this should be done when it is needed. In any case, the value labels should be re-entered to reflect the new version of the variable (so that 1 should represent 'Strongly agree' and 5 'Strongly disagree', for example).

Entering other types of data – not Likert scale items – is relatively straightfor-ward. For any continuous (ratio or interval) data, the number can be entered directly.

For categorical data (whether ordinal or nominal), codes should be given to each category, and data entered (including the value labels) accordingly. In either case, there may be the need to transform or recode some variables; for example, collapsing the values of a nominal variable into fewer categories to enable more sensible analysis (e.g. recoding all four UK countries into a new single nationality code to compare against other non-UK countries). This can be done using similar recoding procedures to those described above; once again, in SPSS it is advisable to use the 'Recode into different variables' option so that the original data are retained.

Sometimes open text data may be included in questionnaires also. The analysis of such data requires more qualitative techniques and is not included in this book; however, most software will allow you to store such data within the same data set (e.g. within SPSS text is stored in a type of variable known as a 'string variable').

One of the most important things to learn about a data set is when and why it may be incomplete. When responding to questionnaires, some people may choose not to answer certain questions (or may be directed not to answer certain questions). It is important (a) to understand how much missing data you have within your data set, and (b) to know (as far as possible) why the data may be missing. In the latter case, it could be worth using different codes for data that should be missing (e.g. because some respondents were not supposed to answer that particular question), or those just left blank by the respondent for no known reason. In SPSS, it is possible to define 'user missing' values, which are given codes for different reasons for being missing (e.g. 'Not applicable', 'Dropped out of study' or 'Missing for unknown reason'), but are left out of any statistical analysis performed. This differs from those simply left blank, represented in the data file by a '.', which are known as 'system missing' values. (An example of this is shown in the fifth row of Q2.2 in Figure 3.2.)

To discover how many missing values there are for each variable, the quickest way may be to get some summary statistics for the whole data set. Box 3.4 shows how this would be done in SPSS, for example.

Box 3.4   SPSS example - summary statistics

To get a descriptive analysis of all variables in SPSS, the simplest way is to use the 'Descriptives' procedure, which produces some basic descriptive statistics for each variable of interest. The default statistics produced are the number of cases, the minimum and maximum, and the mean and standard deviation for each variable, although some other statistics are also available as options.

The 'Descriptives' procedure requires going to the 'Analyze' menu, and then choosing 'Descriptive Statistics' > 'Descriptives'. You can choose all of the variables for the procedure, amend the output produced by changing the 'Options' if required, and then click 'OK' to run. The output will look something like the following:

(Continued)

(Continued)

Descriptive Statistics

	N	Minimum	Maximum	Mean	Std. Deviation
idno	703	90007	99253	94879.11	2013.813
sex	701	0	1	.22	.417
age	702	19	83	42.87	10.092
wkdem1	699	1	5	3.02	1.248
wkdem2	697	1	5	2.76	1.285
wkdem3	699	1	5	2.62	1.262
wkdem4	698	1	5	2.53	1.315
wkdem5	695	1	5	2.38	1.268
wkdem6	606	1	5	2.42	1.295
rolecla1	697	1	5	3.60	1.064
rolecla2	696	1	5	3.51	.951
rolecla3	699	1	5	4.35	.780
rolecla4	697	1	5	3.83	.962
rolecla5	699	1	5	4.08	.942

Figure 3.5

Reprint Courtesy of International Business Machines Corporation, © International Business Machines Corporation

In this example, we can see the first few rows of the table produced. The first numerical column ('N') gives the number of cases for each variable. For most variables these are close to 700, but for one variable (wkdem6) there are only 606 cases – meaning that nearly 100 respondents have no recorded value for that question. It might be that there is a good, known, reason for this, but if not it would be important to try to understand why – because any subsequent analysis using this item will be on a smaller, possibly biased, sample.

Note that descriptive statistics for nominal variables do not generally make sense, so these would typically be excluded from such analyses. For binary variables, however, it is still possible to glean some useful information from this, particularly if it is coded with values 0 and 1 – so, in this example, the variable 'sex' has a mean of 0.22, meaning that 22% of the cases have value 1 (male), and the rest, 78%, are female.

The descriptive statistics procedure can also be useful for other reasons. The default option in SPSS, as demonstrated in Box 3.4, gives not just the number of valid cases for each variable, but the minimum and maximum, as well as the mean and standard deviation. These can be useful for data cleaning and checking; for example, if we know that the minimum and maximum possible values of a variable should be 1 and 5 respectively, then if we see a value of 0 or something greater than 5, we know there has been an error. This enables us to go back and check the data more carefully, and is another reason for having an ID number as the first variable in the file. Likewise, if we see a mean or standard deviation that doesn't tally with what we would expect (e.g. a standard deviation of 0, which would imply everyone having the same value), this should prompt us to look at the raw data and discover what (if anything) has gone wrong.

Even if this procedure does not lead us to any specific problems, it is a good idea to check any manual data entry anyway. For a subset of the data (either randomly chosen selection, or for example every 10th case), compare the entered data with that from the original questionnaire. If there are any mistakes then other cases may have to be checked too. The quality of the research you do is limited by the quality of the data you use: if there are errors here, then the research findings will not be reliable!

3.3 DEFINING MULTI-ITEM SCALES: FACTOR ANALYSIS

Factor analysis is a technique – or, more accurately, a set of techniques – that is used to establish the validity of scales; to demonstrate that the different items of a multi-item scale 'belong' together, but also that they are different from other scales.

Factor analysis might not be necessary for every project. If you are using very well-established scales, that are clearly different in content from each other, then you may proceed directly to the reliability analysis. However, if you are using similar scales for different variables, or are using scales of dubious quality (e.g. those that have not been used in a similar context before), then some form of factor analysis is required.

There are two different forms of factor analysis: exploratory factor analysis (EFA) and confirmatory factor analysis (CFA). EFA is an exploratory procedure that searches for relationships among the variables (items), and assigns items to scales (factors) purely on the basis of these relationships. It should be used whenever there is any doubt over which item belongs on which scale – for example, if closely related new scales are being used, or when it is uncertain whether a construct contains one dimension or more than one. For instance, you may have a set of items measuring customer satisfaction, but it may be unclear whether 'customer satisfaction' is one overall construct that should be considered as a whole, or whether there are two related but separate dimensions (e.g. satisfaction with products and satisfaction with service). In this situation EFA would help determine whether the data support one or two dimensions.

CFA uses more advanced statistical techniques to confirm whether a specified assignment of items to scales agrees with the relationships between items (correlations) that exist in the data set. It compares the actual relationships between items with the relationships that are suggested by the hypothesized structure, and in doing this it assesses how well the data 'fit' the model – in other words, to what extent the hypothesized relationships are consistent with the observed relationships. If scales are being developed for a first time, both EFA and CFA should be used, but on different samples of data.

Whether or not factor analysis is needed, and what type, are important decisions and sometimes people may disagree. Many experts believe that using only CFA is preferable whenever there is an *a priori* belief about what items belong to what scale (see for example Levine et al., 2006). This is because random fluctuations in the data may lead to an alternative structure being found by EFA, when the hypothesized structure is still valid. However, EFA is desirable whenever the assignment of items to scales is in doubt, including when related scales are being used for the first time or in a new context.

Box 3.5 gives some decision criteria about what type of factor analysis (if any) should be done in different circumstances. Note that this is also somewhat dependent on sample size: both EFA and CFA require a fairly large sample size in order to work properly. What 'large' means depends on the specific situation, but a good rule of thumb is that a minimum of ten cases per item included in the analysis, or a minimum of 200 (whichever is the greater) should be required (Thompson, 2004). So, for example, if a CFA was needed for three scales of eight items each, the minimum sample size required would be $3 \times 8 \times 10 = 240$. If an EFA was needed to sort out twelve items, though, a minimum of 200 (as this is greater than $12 \times 10 = 120$) would be required.

Box 3.5   Which type of factor analysis should you use?

Table 3.1

If using any new/amended scales:

> *If sample size permits*, split the sample into two random sub-samples, and run EFA and CFA separately. If you have multiple samples, running EFA and CFA on the separate samples is even better as it prevents sampling bias affecting both sets of results.

> *Otherwise:*

>> If you have clearly different scales and items obviously belong to one or another, use CFA.

>> If there is any ambiguity, or there are no pre-defined scales, use EFA.

If using only published scales (without amendment, and with good reliability/validity in published version):

> *Are scales likely to be highly correlated (e.g. a correlation of above 0.50)?*

>> If no, then no need for factor analysis.

>> If so, then use CFA.

If sample size permits, sometimes it can be useful to split the sample randomly into two sections, and perform EFA on one half and CFA on the other. This effectively enables both the exploratory and confirmatory work to be conducted on the same sample – however, generally this would require at least 400 cases, or more if over 20 items were being examined, in order to be able to do this.

Methods for conducting EFA and CFA are described in Chapter 4, with examples in Chapter 5 and some further discussion of issues around them in Chapter 6.

3.4 SCALE RELIABILITY

In order to confirm that a multi-item scale can be used without fear of measurement error, it is necessary to check its internal consistency as a form of reliability. As described in Chapter 2, this is most commonly done by calculating Cronbach's alpha. This is undertaken separately for each scale.

A full description of how this can be undertaken in SPSS will be given in Chapter 4. However, it is important to note that all items included in a reliability analysis should have the same 'valence' – that is, a higher score should always represent a higher level of the construct being measured. So, for example, if measuring job satisfaction, a high score on each item should correspond to being more satisfied. If measuring work pressure, then a high score on each item should correspond to having more pressure. This may require some items being recoded before being included in the analysis if this was not done at an earlier point.

If the reliability is found to be insufficient (below 0.70 or 0.80 – see Chapter 6 for a discussion of what constitutes acceptable reliability) then some amendments have to be made. There are two main methods of achieving this. First, items could be omitted from the scale to help improve the reliability. This can sometimes work, but you need to be careful that by omitting items you are not changing the meaning or emphasis of the whole scale. Second, if exploratory factor analysis has not been conducted on the data, then this would be an opportune time to do it: it may be that there are actually sub-dimensions of the scale that had not previously been thought of, and that these should be considered as separate scales. If neither approach helps, then unfortunately there is little that can be done: either proceed with the unreliable scale but with the caveat of considerable limitations, or drop the scale entirely from your analysis.

3.5 CREATING OVERALL SCALE SCORES

Once you have a set of items that have been shown to belong to a scale, and you have checked their internal consistency is satisfactory, you can calculate the overall 'scale score' – this is usually the mean of the scores of the individual items (although sometimes the sum is used instead: if there are no missing values then the two methods are equivalent).

Most software will have a straightforward way of creating a new variable in this way. The method for doing it in SPSS is shown in Box 3.6. The only difficult decision at this point is: what should you do about any missing data? Is it acceptable to create a scale score for a respondent if not all of the individual items are present?

There are different possible approaches to this. One would be to only use complete data; that is, if an individual respondent misses any item, they should not have a score for the overall scale. Sometimes missing values might not matter so much, particularly if the scale contains many items. A good compromise is a decision based on reliability: if the scale reliability is good (> 0.80), then a minimum of 75% of the items should be present in order to create an overall scale score (e.g. six items in an eight-item scale; five items in a six-item scale; or all three items in a three-item scale). In this situation, a mean score based only on those items that are present is likely to be a good estimate of the overall variable for that individual. If the reliability is below 0.80, however, then all items should be required in order to create the overall scale score.

Box 3.6   SPSS example – creating overall scale scores

To create a new variable in SPSS you need to use the 'Compute Variable' procedure, which can be found in the 'Transform' menu. You can then specify the name of the new variable (along with its type and label), and a numeric expression indicating what form the new variable should take.

The expression can either be typed in, or put in using the variable list and other tools available. Either way, the expression should include the keyword MEAN (it doesn't need to be in capital letters), and then in brackets a list of all the items, separated by commas. For example, if the required score is the mean of items Var1, Var2, Var3, Var4 and Var5, then the expression would be:

MEAN(Var1, Var2, Var3, Var4, Var5)

(N.B. It doesn't matter whether there are spaces after the commas or not.)

In order to specify that a minimum number of items need to be present in order to calculate the mean score, you can add .x after MEAN, where x is the required number of items. So if we require at least four of the five items above to be present, the expression would be:

MEAN.4(Var1, Var2, Var3, Var4, Var5)

Whenever you create a new scale score, be sure to label it correctly, and save the data file!

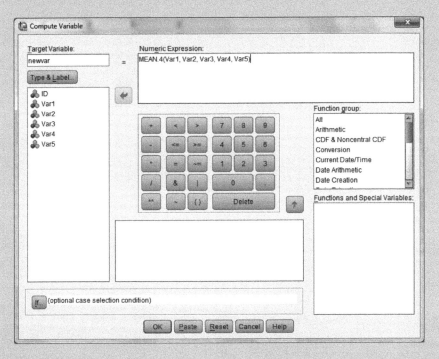

Figure 3.6

Reprint Courtesy of International Business Machines Corporation, © International Business Machines Corporation

This mean score is then used as the variable representing the construct in all your future analysis: generally there is no need to use the individual items any further.

3.6 FURTHER ANALYSIS OF SURVEY DATA

Once you have created overall scale scores, it is likely that you will wish to analyse these in the manner of any variables, whether or not they come from surveys: that is, in either a descriptive/exploratory or inferential way, and using appropriate tools for the requirements of the analysis. Table 3.2 suggests some of the likely statistical tests that you might want to do for either comparing two variables (a single dependent variable (DV) and a single independent variable (IV)), or for more complex relationships (more than one IV). All of these methods are described in much more detail in the book in this series by Scherbaum and Shockley (2015) – this is recommended as further reading for those who wish to conduct any of these tests.

Table 3.2   Some standard statistical tests

	DV is …		
	continuous (normal)	continuous (non-normal), count or ordinal	binary
Simple relationships (one IV)			
To compare two variables (continuous IV)	Correlation (Pearson)	Correlation (Spearman/Kendall)	Logistic regression
Test for the difference between two groups	Independent samples t-test	Mann-Whitney U-test	Chi-squared
Test for the difference between more than two groups	One-way ANOVA	Kruksal-Wallis test	Chi-squared
Test for the difference within individuals (two observations)	Paired-samples t-test	Wilcoxon signed-ranks test	Chi-squared
Test for the difference within individuals (three or more observations)	Repeated Measures ANOVA	Friedman test	–
More complex relationships (two or more IVs, including control variables)			
To compare variables (continuous and/or categorical IVs)	Multiple regression	–	Logistic regression
Test for the difference between two or more groups	ANCOVA	–	Logistic regression
Test for the difference within individuals (two or more observations)	Repeated Measures ANCOVA	–	–

3.7 CHAPTER SUMMARY

In this chapter we have covered the basic procedure for the start of the survey data analysis process, from the point where the data have been collected, through to the point where it is ready for regular analysis (e.g. hypothesis testing). In doing so we have described in more detail the stages of preparing data, including recoding variables and calculating overall scale scores. We have also examined the rationale for different types of factor analysis, and the procedure for conducting reliability analysis. However, the detail of these methods – the heart of good analysis of multi-item scale data – will be covered in Chapter 4.

CHAPTER REFERENCES

Levine, T., Hullett, C.R., Turner, M.M. and Lapinski, M.K. (2006) The desirability of using confirmatory factor analysis on published scales. *Communication Research Reports*, 23(4), 309–314.

Scherbaum, C. and Shockley, K. (2015) *Analysing Quantitative Data for Business and Management Students*. London: Sage.

Thompson, B. (2004) *Exploratory and Confirmatory Factor Analysis*. Washington, DC: American Psychological Association.

4

CONDUCTING CLASSICAL TEST
THEORY ANALYSES

4.1 CHAPTER OVERVIEW

In the previous chapter we saw the steps needed for preliminary analysis and preparation of multi-item scales. Some of these steps (e.g. recoding variables, calculating scale scores) were easily accomplished with a straightforward procedure, particularly if using SPSS. However, some of the steps require a lot more care and decision-making. In this chapter we run through some of the key procedures (reliability analysis, exploratory and confirmatory factor analysis), outlining how they should be approached, what the key decisions are, and how you would go about performing and interpreting the analysis. The description of techniques should allow you to conduct some of the analyses in SPSS, although for factor analysis (whether exploratory factor analysis in SPSS or confirmatory factor analysis in Amos) further reading will be recommended to accompany the basic introduction presented here.

4.2 EXPLORATORY FACTOR ANALYSIS

As described in Chapter 3, exploratory factor analysis is a method used when there are several questionnaire items (variables) representing a number (one or more) of underlying constructs – the things you want the measurements to represent – and the aim is to determine which items should go with each construct.

The principle behind exploratory factor analysis relates back closely to the principles of classical test theory described in Chapter 2. According to CTT, a measurement of an item, (x_i), is composed of the true score (t_i) and an error (e_i):

$$x_i = t_i + e_i$$

Factor analysis assumes that the true score, t_i, is the value of an underlying (latent) construct - that is, the concept that is being measured by a combination of items (for instance, continuing the example of previous chapters, this could be extraversion). Therefore for each item that is part of a multi-item scale - say, x_1, x_2, x_3, x_4 - each would have the same value of t and each error term comprising both error unique to that item, and random error:

$$x_{1i} = t_i + e_{1i}$$

$$x_{2i} = t_i + e_{2i}$$

$$x_{3i} = t_i + e_{3i}$$

$$x_{4i} = t_i + e_{4i}$$

The goal of exploratory factor analysis is twofold: to detect how many such underlying constructs there are, and to identify which items 'belong' to which construct.

Technically, the EFA procedure scrutinizes the correlations between all of the variables, and uses these to identify a new variable ('factor') constructed of combinations of all of the original variables, which accounts for as much of the variation in the data as possible. It then identifies a second factor that accounts for as much of the remaining variation, and then a third, and so on until all of the variation is explained (which will happen when as many factors have been identified as there are variables). The job of the researcher is to determine how many of these factors are needed to account for a substantial enough amount of variation, and then what these factors mean.

In SPSS, the factor analysis procedure is accessed via the 'Analyze' menu, then going to 'Dimension Reduction' > 'Factor'. You then choose the variables (items) that are going to be analysed (see Figure 4.1). A number of other options need to be specified, however, and to explain what these mean, it is worth considering the different stages of the factor analysis process.

The factor analysis procedure does everything in one go, although there are four real stages as part of it:

1. Examining whether all items should be included.
2. Determining the ideal number of factors to be used.
3. Extracting factors.
4. Rotating and interpreting the extracted factors.

In reality they may be done as part of one overall procedure, but we now look at each of these in turn.

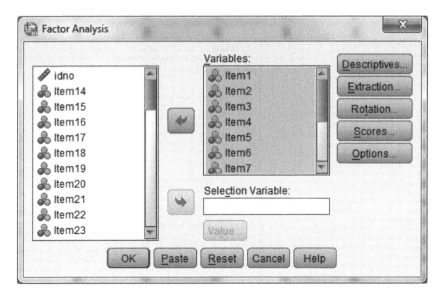

Figure 4.1   Specifying a factor analysis in SPSS

Reprint Courtesy of International Business Machines Corporation, © International Business Machines Corporation

4.2.1 Examining whether all items should be included

The first and simplest stage is to examine whether all of the variables (items) should
be included in the analysis. This is the answer to the question: do they really share
enough in common with the other items? According to CTT, a shared true score with
other items as part of the same construct would be essential, and the variation of
the error terms should be relatively small: therefore we would expect a reasonable
amount of variation shared between an item and the rest of the data (or, to put it
another way, a relatively small amount of variance unique to each item).

   This is observed via the communalities – a measure of the variance of each item that is
shared with other items, as opposed to that which is unique. For example, in Figure 4.2, we
see the communalities for an exploratory factor analysis of 13 items from a questionnaire.

   There are two columns: 'Initial' and 'Extraction' communalities. The initial communalities show the amount of the variance of an item that is shared with (or explained
by) the other items. The extraction communalities show the proportion of variance
that can be explained by the extracted factors. In terms of determining whether or
not an item should be included in the analysis, it is the initial communalities that are
the most use. There are no firm cut-offs that should be applied here: different types of
data often yield very different magnitudes of communalities. However, if an item has
a very much lower communality than other items, this suggests it may not belong as
part of the analysis. In the example in Figure 4.2, the lowest communality is 0.183 (for
item 13), which is not very much lower than the next lowest (item 12, 0.212), and there

Communalities

	Initial	Extraction
Item1	.363	.377
Item2	.311	.281
Item3	.429	.456
Item4	.518	.618
Item5	.239	.230
Item6	.381	.375
Item7	.441	.500
Item8	.335	.306
Item9	.522	.598
Item10	.498	.616
Item11	.444	.494
Item12	.212	.236
Item13	.183	.199

Extraction Method: Principal Axis Factoring.

Figure 4.2 Example of communalities from a factor analysis

Reprint Courtesy of International Business Machines Corporation, © International Business Machines Corporation

are no very large gaps in between adjacently sized communalities; therefore there is no suggestion that any items should be excluded.

An overall indicator of whether the data are appropriate for factor analysis can be given by the Kaiser-Meyer-Olkin (KMO) measure of sampling adequacy. This can be requested in SPSS by checking the 'KMO and Bartlett's Test of Sphericity' box under the 'Descriptives' button in the factor analysis procedure. It produces a table including two tests, as indicated in Figure 4.3.

KMO and Bartlett's Test

Kaiser-Meyer-Olkin Measure of Sampling Adequacy.		.854
Bartlett's Test of Sphericity	Approx. Chi-Square	11941.348
	df	78
	Sig.	.000

Figure 4.3 Kaiser-Meyer-Olkin and Bartlett tests

Reprint Courtesy of International Business Machines Corporation, © International Business Machines Corporation

The KMO measure is always between 0 and 1; values closer to 1 suggest the data are more appropriate for factor analysis, with 0.6 often seen as a minimum appropriate level. The Bartlett's Test of Sphericity simply tests a null hypothesis that the variables are completely uncorrelated with each other – as long as the p-value (the 'Sig.' value on the final row) is significant (i.e. $p < .05$), this suggests there is not a problem.

4.2.2 Determining the ideal number of factors to be used

The number of factors that should be used is a very important but not always straightforward decision. Sometimes, for example, two factors may be very closely related to each other, and it may not be obvious whether they should actually be considered as two separate constructs or one. For example, some research has suggested that the psychological concept of 'burnout' is the inverse of the concept of 'work engagement', and therefore these would form one overall construct. Other research has suggested these are not opposites, but actually represent different constructs. Therefore the goal of this stage of the analysis is to determine the best 'solution' to the data; that is, how many factors should be interpreted as separate constructs (or 'retained').

The reason the decision is sometimes difficult is that there is no one ideal method for determining the actual number of underlying factors. Two methods (the Kaiser criterion and the scree test) are common and fairly easy to apply; a third method (parallel analysis) often produces better results but is not so easy to apply in most software.

To understand how to apply and interpret these methods, it is first important to understand the concept of an 'eigenvalue'. This is a mathematical term, meaning the part of the variance that is particular to a vector (from the German 'eigen' meaning 'own' or 'individual'), and in the context of factor analysis it is an indication of how much of the total variation is accounted for by a factor (each factor having its own eigenvalue; the first factor would have the largest eigenvalue, the second factor the next largest, and so on). The eigenvalues are scaled such that the sum of all eigenvalues (if all possible factors are used) is equal to the number of variables in the analysis – or, to put it another way, an eigenvalue of 1 would be equivalent to the average amount of variation accounted for by a single variable.

This explains the rationale behind the first decision method – the Kaiser criterion. This method – which is the default decision method used by some software, including SPSS – automatically chooses to retain the factors with eigenvalues greater than 1. That is, each factor as part of the solution should contribute more of the variation than an average item would.

Although this is intuitively appealing in some ways, is straightforward to apply, and sometimes produces the best solution, it has two significant flaws. First, simply having an eigenvalue greater than 1 does not, in itself, mean that a factor is sufficiently meaningful. Even in completely random data – variables generated by chance rather than due to underlying constructs – some 'factors' produced via factor analysis will have eigenvalues greater than 1. Second, it is a fairly arbitrary cut-off; there is nothing magical about an eigenvalue of 1, and a factor with an eigenvalue of 1.05 would be relatively indistinguishable from one with an eigenvalue of 0.95.

For these reasons it is usually thought better to examine the relative eigenvalues of the factors, and to retain factors that have clearly higher eigenvalues than subsequent factors. This is most easily decided via the 'scree test'. This uses a plot of successive eigenvalues – called a scree plot because it often resembles the rock formation towards the bottom of a cliff or steep slope, known as scree – to provide a visual clue as to how many factors should be retained.

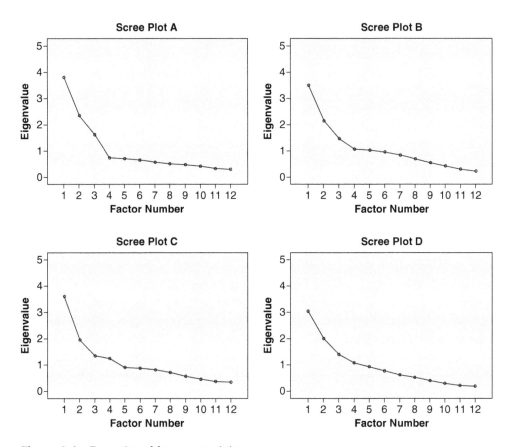

Figure 4.4   Examples of four scree plots

For a set of examples, see Figure 4.4. Plot A shows a typical situation: a small number of factors have eigenvalues substantially greater than 1, and this part of the plot shows a clear 'cliff face' with the first three points forming part of this. The fourth point, however, is substantially lower than the third, but barely higher than the fifth. In fact, the fourth point is a sort of elbow in the pattern: where the 'scree' starts. This is a relatively clear-cut example: the first three factors would be retained, as the fourth and subsequent factors do not add enough to the variation explained. In addition, the first three factors have eigenvalues greater than 1, whereas the remainder all have eigenvalues below one.

Plot B shows a similar pattern; however, in this case, the fourth and fifth eigenvalues are also greater than 1. Nevertheless, because of the shape of the plot, it would still be preferable to retain the first three eigenvalues only.

Plot C shows a different type of situation: there are two possible places where the plot levels off: after the third and fifth points. There is a drop between the fourth and fifth eigenvalues, although it is small compared with the drops after the first and second. To complicate matters slightly further, the third eigenvalue is slightly above one, and the fourth slightly below one. In this situation, it could be that a two-factor solution would be preferable, or that a four-factor solution would be. It is certainly not the three-factor solution, however, which is what would be given automatically by software (e.g. SPSS) using the Kaiser criterion. To decide between the two-factor and four-factor solutions, it would be advisable to try both: proceed with two different solutions, each gained by specifying a different number of factors to be extracted as part of the analysis. The choice between the two would then come down to which provided the better theoretical interpretation (see section 4.2.4).

Plot D shows a situation where there is no clear change of direction in the scree plot at all. This is the most difficult situation to deal with, as it suggests there may not be a fixed set of factors underlying the data, and therefore factor analysis may not be appropriate: it may be preferable to use principal components analysis instead (see section 4.2.5). Nevertheless, if it is necessary to proceed with the analysis, two methods may be used: trying solutions with different numbers of factors, and seeing which has the most sensible theoretical interpretation; or using parallel analysis.

Parallel analysis is a more sophisticated method of choosing the number of factors that improves on the arbitrary nature of the Kaiser criterion, but is more objective than the scree test. It uses the fact that, simply by chance, some factors that are unimportant are likely to have eigenvalues greater than 1; it simulates random data for the number of cases and variables involved, and selects out however many factors have higher eigenvalues than the equivalent factors in the simulated data.

Although a good criterion, this method is not currently available in SPSS and is therefore not widely used at present. More information can be found by referring to Thompson and Daniel (1996), or using the resources at https://people.ok.ubc.ca/brioconn/nfactors/nfactors.html.

Another potentially useful indicator of the success of a solution is the percentage of the total variance explained by the factors extracted. There are no absolute rules about how much should be explained: authors have suggested anywhere between 50% and 90%, but in truth it can vary hugely by the type of data used, and sometimes even below 50% is adequate. If a specific factor structure is expected to account for all of the items in the analysis, a larger percentage should be expected.

Figure 4.5 shows the variance explained section of the SPSS output for an analysis where two factors appears to be the best solution. Note that there are three sections to the table. The first section, 'Initial Eigenvalues', refers to the overall eigenvalues on the whole data set. The 'Total' column gives the actual eigenvalues (note that two are well above 1, with several others falling just below 1); the second column expresses these as a percentage of variance explained (this is equal to the eigenvalue divided by the number of items, 13, multiplied by 100), and third column shows the cumulative percentage (so that the first two factors explain 48.7% of the total variance between them).

The second section, 'Extraction Sums of Squared Loadings', gives similar information, but only for the two factors extracted (to be explained in section 4.2.3). The values here are lower, because they are based only on the shared variance, and ignore variance that is unique to particular items. The third section, 'Rotation Sums of Squared Loadings', gives the equivalent eigenvalues after the rotation (which will be explained in section 4.2.4). Note that the variance here is more equally shared between the factors: the rotation assists our interpretation by spreading the variation more equitably across the factors.

Total Variance Explained

Factor	Initial Eigenvalues			Extraction Sums of Squared Loadings			Rotation Sums of Squared Loadings[a]
	Total	% of Variance	Cumulative %	Total	% of Variance	Cumulative%	Total
1	4.440	34.157	34.157	3.865	29.729	29.729	3.441
2	1.891	14.546	48.703	1.419	10.918	40.647	2.705
3	.998	7.676	56.379				
4	.883	6.793	63.172				
5	.817	6.282	69.454				
6	.706	5.431	74.885				
7	.626	4.817	79.702				
8	.570	4.383	84.084				
9	.512	3.941	88.025				
10	.475	3.651	91.677				
11	.436	3.356	95.033				
12	.340	2.612	97.645				
13	.306	2.355	100.000				

Extraction Method: Principal Axis Factoring.

a. When factors are correlated, sums of squared loadings cannot be added to obtain a total variance.

Figure 4.5 Variance explained table from SPSS output

4.2.3 Extracting factors

The third part of the process is to actually extract the factors that have been decided upon: that is, to identify what the particular combinations of items are that account for the maximum amount of variation possible. Mathematically, there are different ways of doing this.

The most common method, called 'principal axis factoring' in SPSS, is the traditional method, based wholly on the classical test theory idea of factor analysis described earlier in this chapter. An alternative method is using maximum likelihood: this is a method of choosing factors that have the highest 'likelihood' value; that is, that they give the best overall fit to the data. Maximum likelihood can produce some additional statistics, but is only valid when the data are normally distributed. If there is deviation from normality – as is often the case with survey items – then principal axis factoring is more accurate. Therefore we proceed on the assumption that principal axis factoring is the method to be used. Another extraction method that is a bit different is principal components analysis: technically this is different from factor analysis, although it is often classified under the same set of procedures. This is discussed more in section 4.2.5.

In SPSS, the different extraction options can be chosen by using the 'Extraction' button in the factor analysis procedure. As shown in Figure 4.6, a drop-down menu is used for choosing the extraction method; a scree plot can be chosen with a tick-box; and the decision criterion for the number of factors can also be specified here (either based on a minimum eigenvalue – by default, 1, which is the Kaiser criterion – or a fixed number of factors, to be specified by the user).

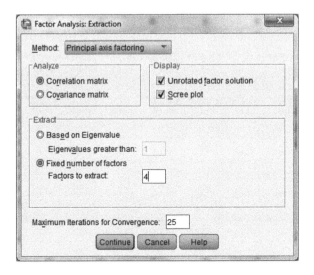

Figure 4.6   Specifying extraction options

Reprint Courtesy of International Business Machines Corporation, © International Business Machines Corporation

Unfortunately, the extracted factors are not generally possible to interpret – at least, not directly. This is because they are described in a mathematical way that is not aligned with our interpretation of the items themselves. To produce an interpretable solution, we first need to rotate the factors.

4.2.4 Rotating and interpreting the extracted factors

Rotating factors is essential in order to produce an interpretable solution. This procedure changes the basis of the factors – in mathematical terms it swivels the axes for each – so that they can be easily interpreted in terms of the original items. These options can be changed with the 'Rotation' button in the factor analysis procedure in SPSS.

There are several different methods of rotation possible. Broadly, these can be categorized into 'orthogonal' and 'oblique' rotations. Orthogonal rotations ensure that each rotated factor is orthogonal to (i.e. uncorrelated with) each factor that goes before. These are useful in situations where you want to ensure the factors are as different from each other as possible. There are different types of orthogonal rotation, three of which are offered in SPSS (Varimax, Quartimax, Equimax). These all have slightly different methods for maximizing the variance between factors, but Varimax is often considered the most appropriate and is certainly the most popular.

Oblique rotations, however, allow factors to be correlated, and are therefore preferred whenever the underlying constructs are expected to be related to each other. This includes most cases of multiple multi-item scales in organizational or other social research, and therefore an oblique rotation should be the usual option (Conway and Huffcutt, 2003). SPSS offers two versions of oblique rotations – Direct Oblimin and Promax. Like the different orthogonal rotations, they offer different approaches to the same problem, and either can be used, but Direct Oblimin is generally preferred for survey data. As shown in Figure 4.7, if you choose this then the Delta (a parameter that controls the amount of obliqueness allowed) should usually be set at zero.

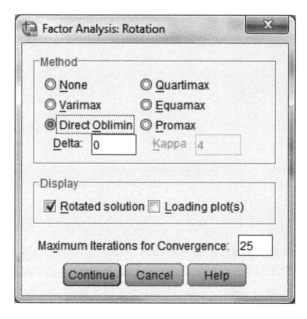

Figure 4.7   Specifying rotation options

Reprint Courtesy of International Business Machines Corporation, © International Business Machines Corporation

The interpretation of the rotated solution, however, is often quite difficult. The rotated factor matrix – called a pattern matrix if an oblique rotation has been used – gives factor loadings for each item on each factor. Crudely, these are equivalent to the correlation between an item and a factor, and therefore have values of less than 1 (and greater than −1). You should identify which items belong to each factor by observing which factor loadings are larger than a given value (0.5 is often used, although 0.4 may be used instead: negative values which are less than −0.5 or −0.4 respectively would also count).

This may seem a relatively easy thing to do; however, two issues complicate the matter:

1. Items with high loadings on multiple factors ('Cross loading').
2. Arbitrariness of loading cut-offs.

The issue of items loading strongly on more than one factor is particularly troubling, as according to the factor analysis model using classical test theory, each item should be strongly related to one factor only. Therefore if an item has high loadings on more than one factor in a solution that is otherwise acceptable, it is recommended that the cross-loading item is dropped from future analysis. If too many items cross-load in this way, it suggests that the factor structure retained is not supportable.

Ideally, we would observe some items with very high loadings on a factor (e.g. well above 0.5), and all of the others with very low loadings (e.g. below 0.3). However, in reality this does not always happen – there are sometimes items in between 0.3 and 0.5, and sometimes these may cross-load onto multiple factors at this level. There is often a judgement to be made (involving some experience and subjectivity) about whether these items should be retained on one factor or dropped.

As an example, compare the two pattern matrices in Figures 4.8 and 4.9. In Figure 4.8, there is a clear separation of factors: items 17 to 21 have very high loadings (above 0.7) on factor 1, and negligible loadings on factor 2; items 14 to 16 have very high loadings on factor 2, but negligible loadings on factor 1. Therefore it should be a relatively straightforward decision to choose items 14 to 16 as one factor, and items 17 to 21 as another.

In Figure 4.9, however, this is less clear. Although there are some items that load clearly on one of the two factors, there are others that do not have high loadings on either (e.g. item 5), and others that have relatively high loadings on both (item 2). In this scenario it is likely that either a different number of factors would be used, or if two factors is clearly the correct choice, then these items would probably be dropped from further analysis (as they cannot be uniquely associated with one factor).

The interpretation of the pattern matrix can be made easier by using an additional feature available in SPSS. Factor loadings with values less than a certain absolute value can be suppressed – that is, in the pattern matrix they will appear as blanks. For example, you can choose to suppress any values less than 0.3 (or less than −0.3 if they are negative). This is done by choosing the 'Options' button in the factor analysis procedure, and checking the 'Suppress small coefficients' box, specifying the value below which they are to be suppressed (see Figure 4.10 for an example).

Pattern Matrix[a]

	Factor	
	1	2
Item14	-.065	.732
Item15	.034	.916
Item16	.163	.701
Item17	.862	-.027
Item18	.927	-.053
Item19	.851	-.024
Item20	.755	.074
Item21	.704	100

Figure 4.8   Example of a clearly defined pattern matrix

Reprint Courtesy of International Business Machines Corporation, © International Business Machines Corporation

Pattern Matrix[a]

	Factor	
	1	2
Item1	.590	-.058
Item2	-.431	.478
Item3	.726	.217
Item4	.069	.809
Item5	.283	-.296
Item6	.177	-.524
Item7	.286	-.549
Item8	.502	-.111
Item9	.794	.060
Item10	.140	.826
Item11	.689	-.034
Item12	-.385	.186
Item13	.461	.046

Figure 4.9   Example of a less clearly defined pattern matrix

Reprint Courtesy of International Business Machines Corporation, © International Business Machines Corporation

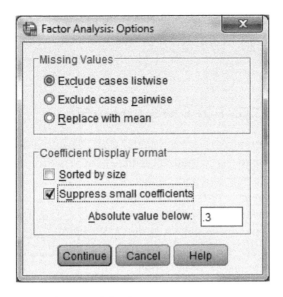

Figure 4.10   Making the pattern matrix clearer

Reprint Courtesy of International Business Machines Corporation, © International Business Machines Corporation

This will generate an easier-to-view pattern matrix – Figure 4.11 shows the same pattern matrix as Figure 4.8, but with small values suppressed. It is clear now to see the 'pattern' in the data – the items that load strongly on each factor are easily visible. Note that just because a loading is not suppressed it does not mean it is a strong loading: it is recommended to show all loadings above 0.3, even though 0.4 or 0.5 are more usually

Pattern Matrix[a]

	Factor	
	1	2
Item14		.732
Item15		.916
Item16		.701
Item17	.862	
Item18	.927	
Item19	.851	
Item20	.755	
Item21	.704	

Figure 4.11   The revised pattern matrix

Reprint Courtesy of International Business Machines Corporation, © International Business Machines Corporation

chosen as cut-offs for strong loadings. This is because whichever cut-off is used is arbitrary, and a value just less than that (e.g. 0.396) might be considered to have a strong loading if it is not so different from the other strong loadings on that factor.

4.3 PRINCIPAL COMPONENTS ANALYSIS

A closely related method to exploratory factor analysis, and one which is sometimes referred to as factor analysis (although technically it is different, as it uses different assumptions), is principal components analysis (PCA). Like EFA it examines the correlations between variables to detect underlying patterns. However, unlike EFA, it is not based on classical test theory – i.e. it does not assume that an item is composed of an underlying construct plus some error. As such PCA is better used for 'data reduction' – an attempt to reduce a larger number of variables to a smaller number for pragmatic purposes. EFA is preferable whenever there is an *a priori* reason to believe that a number of theoretical constructs underlie the responses to a survey.

The distinction between EFA and PCA, and recommendations about how and when to use them, are further discussed in Chapter 6.

4.4 CONFIRMATORY FACTOR ANALYSIS

Confirmatory factor analysis – commonly known by the abbreviation CFA – is a technique to check whether an expected factor structure (i.e. the way that items fit within constructs) is consistent with the data. It examines what correlations are actually found between variables, and compares this with the correlations that would be expected if the hypothesized structure were perfectly true.

Say, for example, you have ten items that you believe belong to three constructs – let's say not only the three items for extraversion which we have seen before, but also two other personality dimensions, agreeableness and neuroticism (three items each). Under classical test theory the three personality constructs are the only meaningful things that determine the responses to these questions (any differences from this being due to error); this means that, as a diagram, the relationship between the items and constructs looks like the diagram in Figure 4.12.

The key features of this diagram are that there are three 'latent' variables (extraversion, agreeableness and neuroticism) – variables that are not measured directly but are thought to underlie the responses to the nine questionnaire items (which are 'observed' items, in that they are measured directly). Each questionnaire item included is uniquely associated with one of the latent variables; the arrows from the latent variable to the observed items indicate the factor analysis model under classical test theory that the item's value is largely determined by the latent variable (plus some error). Note also that the three latent variables are correlated, but other than

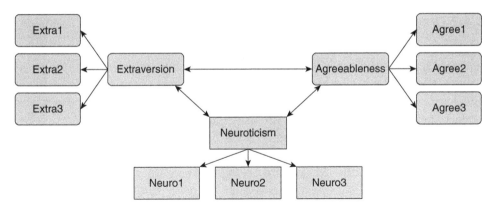

Figure 4.12   Factor structure for nine personality items

this there are no correlations between any of the variables. This enables the analysis to determine what the expected correlations between items might be, once these constraints are taken into account.

In order to test this, we need to compare the model of interest (the model described above, with the constraints applied) with the actual data, to see whether the correlations between items under the constraints are close to the correlations that we observe (or, to put it another way, how well the model 'fits' the data). Unfortunately this is something that cannot be done in SPSS, and so the following sections discuss software that can be used, how the model can be specified in one such software package (Amos), how the model can be evaluated, and how different models can be compared.

4.4.1 Software for conducting CFA

As noted in the previous section, it is not possible to conduct CFA within SPSS. CFA is a specific form of the technique known as 'structural equation modelling' (SEM), and therefore it is best conducted in specialist SEM software.

There are many software packages that can conduct SEM, and therefore CFA. Some of these were developed specifically for the purpose of conducting SEM – such as LISREL, EQS, Mplus and Amos. Others are more general statistical software platforms that have ways of incorporating SEM, such as R and SAS.

Sections 4.4.3 and 4.4.4, which discuss evaluating and comparing models, can be applied to any software. However, the method of specifying the model differs substantially between them. Therefore section 4.4.2 describes the method of specifying the model in one particular software package – Amos. This is chosen because it is distributed with SPSS (and therefore many people with access to SPSS also have access to Amos), and also because the method of specifying the model to be tested involves drawing the model.

4.4.2 Drawing the model

When you open Amos for the first time, you will see something that looks similar to Figure 4.13. This is the blank Amos screen, and it includes three sections. The large, plain section on the right-hand side is the software's 'main drawing board' – this is where you should draw the model, as Amos works from a visual depiction of the model to be tested (most other software uses special programming syntax to specify the model, which can be harder to learn for the beginner).

In order to draw the model, you would first need to know what the model should look like; effectively, you are trying to recreate something that looks similar to the model shown in Figure 4.12, but with some crucial differences (shown later).

To create the drawing itself, you will need to use the 'drawing palette', shown on the left-hand side of the screen in Figure 4.13 – this palette contains icons used to create the drawing, the most commonly used of which are described later. The middle section, in between the palette and the drawing board, is where certain details of the models tested are shown. This can be ignored until you have created and tested at least one model.

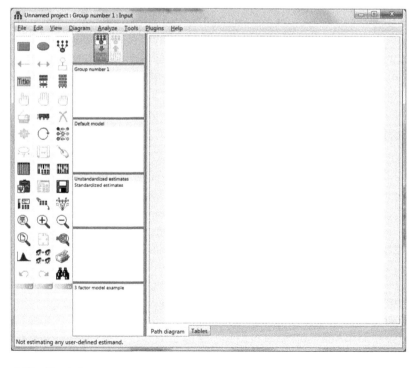

Figure 4.13   Blank Amos screen

Reprint Courtesy of International Business Machines Corporation, © International Business Machines Corporation

If you are using Amos, it is worth familiarizing yourself with some of the particular icons in the drawing palette. Some of the most important ones are as follows:

 This is used to draw an *observed variable* (i.e. one that appears in the data set you are analysing). Click on this icon on the toolbar, then click and drag on the drawing palette to draw the variable.

 This is used to draw a *latent variable* (one that is not in the data set, but that you want to estimate as part of your model). It can be drawn in the same way as an observed variable.

 This can be used to draw a *latent factor* (i.e. a latent variable with several observed variables/items making up the factor, known as indicators). It is particularly useful for CFA. Click and drag to create the latent variable in the same way as above, but then click on the latent variable to add observed variables to it.

 This draws a *regression* path from one variable to another. With the icon selected, click on one variable and drag to another variable.

 This draws a *correlation* between two variables. Particularly useful for CFA.

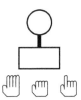 This adds an *error term* to an existing observed variable. Not used so frequently in CFA, but very useful for other types of SEM.

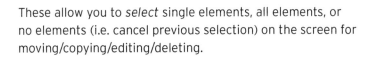 These allow you to *select* single elements, all elements, or no elements (i.e. cancel previous selection) on the screen for moving/copying/editing/deleting.

  These allow you to *copy*, *move* or *delete* elements accordingly.

 This allows you to change the *shape* or size of an existing element.

 This *rotates* the indicators (items) of a latent variable by 90 degrees clockwise.

Figure 4.14 shows how the model described earlier (and shown in Figure 4.12) is translated into an Amos drawing.

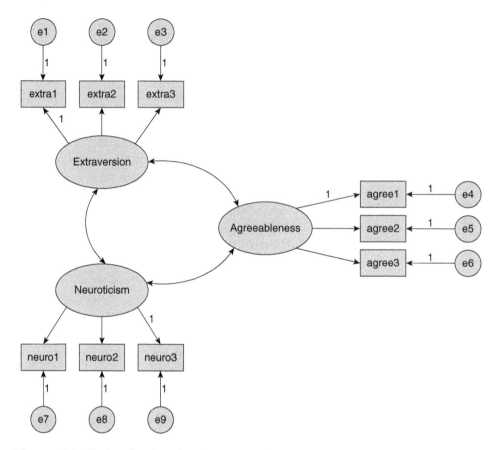

Figure 4.14   Factor structure for nine personality items

There are some key differences between this and the model drawing in Figure 4.12. First, there is a distinction between the latent variables – shown in oval shapes – and the observed variables (items) – shown in rectangles. Second, each item has another circular variable with an arrow going to it, each with a separate name. These are error terms, and account for the error in the factor model as described at the beginning of this chapter. Third, the arrow from each error term, and exactly one of the arrows from each latent variable to an item, is marked with a '1' – these represent constraints on the model that are needed to run a CFA (parameters that are fixed to a certain value: without these, there are too many unknowns and a solution cannot be achieved). The good news is that Amos does each of these three things automatically if these are created using the 'latent factor' drawing tool.

When creating a model involving multiple factors in Amos, therefore, it is sensible to follow these steps:

1. Create your first latent factor by choosing the 'latent factor' icon, and then somewhere towards the centre of the drawing board, clicking and holding/dragging the mouse to

display the latent variable on the screen. By default, a single observed variable (plus error term) is automatically created too. You can add to this now by clicking on the latent factor itself: each click generates a new observed variable. So if this first factor is one with five items, you would click four times in total to generate the five items.

2. Create other latent factors in the same way, or alternatively by selecting, copying and pasting the factor you have already created (items can be added by click-ing on the 'latent factor' icon and then on the latent variable itself, or removed by choosing the 'delete' icon and clicking on both the observed variable to be removed and its corresponding error term).

3. Make the model look neater by (a) rotating factors so that the items go in a different direction using the 'rotate' icon (select the icon, and then click on the relevant factor), (b) selecting all parts of a factor (latent variable, items and error terms – use the single finger version of the 'select' icon, and then click on all of these parts) and moving it around the screen (click on the move icon, and then drag the selected objects around the screen accordingly – then choose the no fingers version of the 'select' icon to unselect everything), and if needed (c) changing the size and shape of any objects by choosing the 'shape' icon and clicking/dragging any objects that need changing.

4. The correlations between latent variables need to be added manually: do this by choosing the double-headed arrow 'correlation' icon, and then dragging from one latent variable to another, until each pair of latent variables is connected. (Note that the curvature of the correlations can also be changed using the 'shape' icon.)

5. Add variable names to each of the variables (latent variables, observed items and error terms). This can be done either by double clicking on a particular variable, or choosing 'Object properties' from the 'Diagram' menu, and then typing in the variable name into the 'Variable name' box. It is important that, for observed vari-ables, these are given exactly the same name that they have in the SPSS data file. For other variables (latent variables and errors) they should not have the same name as a variable in the data set, and each name must be unique.

Before the analysis can be run, two other things need to be done. First, analysis prop-erties can be chosen using the analysis properties icon in the palette, or alternatively by choosing 'Analysis Properties' from the menu. The most important thing to choose is on the 'Output' tab, where you can choose to request 'Standardized estimates' (as shown in Figure 4.15; the reason why will become clear in section 4.4.3).

If your data file contains any missing values among the variables you are analys-ing, then you also have to go to the 'Estimation' tab and select 'Estimate means and intercepts' – this will ensure Amos uses an appropriate procedure for analysing incomplete data (if you do not do this, the analysis will not run).

The other important task is telling Amos which data file you are using. You can choose this using the 'Select data file' icon (the one that looks like a large table of data). The file can then be chosen from those available on your computer, and the analysis can be run using the 'Calculate estimates' icon – the one that looks like an abacus (or alternatively choose this from the 'Analyze' menu).

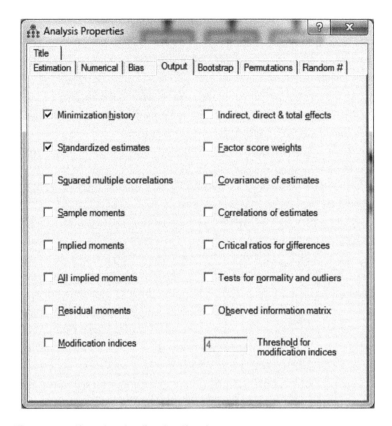

Figure 4.15   Requesting standardized estimates

Reprint Courtesy of International Business Machines Corporation, © International Business Machines Corporation

4.4.3 Interpreting the output

Amos output includes several sections, but there are two key parts for interpreting the results of a CFA. The first part is evaluating the model fit, which can be seen by choosing the 'Model Fit' section on the left-hand side of the output screen (shown in Figure 4.16).

Model fit is evaluated via a series of indices. Many are produced because they all have slightly different meanings and interpretations, and depending on the circumstances some may be preferred. However, for CFA, there are three fit indices that are best to examine:

- CFI (Comparative Fit Index). This should be above 0.90 for good fit, with 0.95 representing excellent fit. Values below 0.80 would be considered completely unacceptable.
- TLI (Tucker-Lewis Index). This is interpreted in the same way as the CFI.
- RMSEA (Root Mean Squared Error of Approximation). This should be below 0.06 for good fit, with values below 0.08 considered adequate. Values above 0.10 would be considered unacceptable.

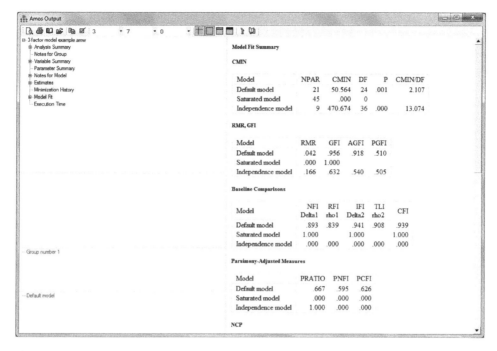

Figure 4.16   Viewing model fit in Amos

Reprint Courtesy of International Business Machines Corporation, © International Business Machines Corporation

In some cases, one or two of these fit indices might show good fit, but the other(s) do not. This indicates that the model is possibly satisfactory but is not ideal.

Box 4.1   Other fit indices

You may see other fit indices quoted in some academic papers. One of these, the Standardized Root Mean Square Residual (SRMR), is considered a good one, and while this is not produced automatically by Amos, it can be found by choosing the SRMR plug-in from the 'Plug Ins' menu before running the analysis (this brings up a separate window in which the index will appear after analysis is run).

Other fit indices may be useful in some circumstances, but not generally for evaluating single models. In particular, the chi-square index (referred to as CMIN in Amos) is thought by many not to be a good evaluation of model fit (and neither is chi-square divided by the degrees of freedom, which is sometimes seen) as the chi-square value is heavily biased by sample size – that is, the same model will have a larger chi-square value if it is based on a larger sample from the same population, which is not helpful when in general larger samples are considered better. However, chi-square can be very useful for comparing models – see section 4.4.4 for more on this.

If the model fit is satisfactory or good, then this suggests the proposed factor structure can be confirmed. If the model fit is not good, however, then it is important to
see how the model might be improved. Even if the fit is good, examining the model in
more depth can be beneficial for various reasons.

The key place to start is by looking at the 'Estimates' section of the output, as
shown in Figure 4.17.

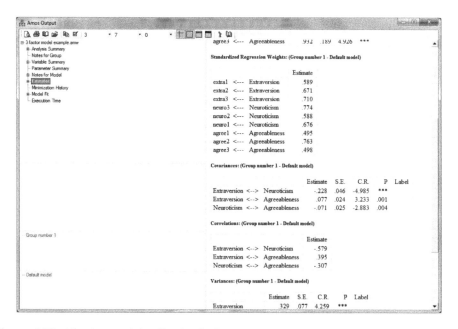

Figure 4.17 Viewing model estimates in Amos

Reprint Courtesy of International Business Machines Corporation, © International Business Machines Corporation

Two sets of figures are particularly of interest here. First, the standardized regression
weights are directly equivalent to the factor loadings from exploratory factor analysis.
Therefore noticing whether any of these is particularly small (or much smaller than
the others at least) may be an indication that an item should not really form part of
the scale. The other set of figures worth examining is the correlations between factors. In Figure 4.17 we see that the correlation with the largest magnitude is between
Extraversion and Neuroticism, with a correlation of −0.579.

This is a large correlation, but probably not too large for these factors to be considered as separate variables. There are two ways we can check this though. The first
way is to use a test put forward by Fornell and Larcker (1981), which compares the factor loadings with the correlations. To check that the factors are suitably distinct, we
calculate the average of the squared factor loadings for each (so in this case we would
take each of the three standardized regression weights for a factor, square them, and

take the mean of these three squared loadings; this is known as the Average Variance Extracted, or AVE). If the AVE for two variables exceeds the square of the correlation between those two factors, then the factors are said to have 'discriminant validity' – in other words, they can be reliably distinguished, even if the correlation is high.

The second method involves a comparison of different models within Amos, and is discussed in section 4.4.4.

4.4.4 Comparing models

Sometimes it is desirable to compare two or more models to see which has a better fit to the data – sometimes these models might represent different factor structures suggested by alternative EFAs – or compare a factor structure from an EFA with one suggested by theory, or simply check that a model is better than an alternative (but credible) model.

The simple way of comparing two models is to run them both, and then see which has the better fit indices. However, this does not tell the whole story. For one thing, a model that is more complex may have better fit, but if it is not substantially better then it might be better to select the more parsimonious (simpler) model. Also, if models are 'nested', then there is a specific test to check whether one is better than the other.

'Nested' in this context has a very specific meaning. If one model is nested within another, then it is possible to get from the first model to the second by adding paths to the model (or, equivalently, by removing constraints, such as a path that is fixed at a certain value). Sometimes nested models may not be obvious: for example, if you were to add a constraint that two latent variables have a correlation of 1 (meaning they are the same variable), then this is a constraint, and this means that all of the items for those two latent variables effectively become part of one larger, new latent variable.

As an example, consider the model shown before (in Figure 4.14). As seen in the previous section, the correlation between Extraversion and Neuroticism was reasonably high. Therefore it might be desirable to compare the fit of the original model with the fit of a second model where the Extraversion items and the Neuroticism items were associated with just one latent variable (factor), equivalent to the previous model but with the correlation between the factors fixed at 1. See Figure 4.18 for the new, alternative model.

The fit of this model can be calculated in the usual way. However, there is formal test to see whether this better represents the data than the previous model. It involves comparing the chi-square values (CMIN) from the two models, and also the number of degrees of freedom in the two models (degrees of freedom is a technical term indicating how many more changes could be made to the model before it would fit any data perfectly).

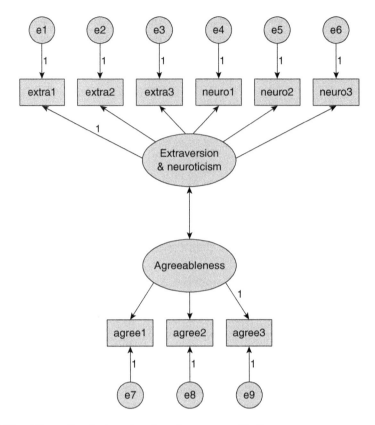

Figure 4.18 Alternative factor structure for personality items

The chi-square values from the original model (Figure 4.14) was 50.564, with 24 degrees of freedom. The chi-square values from this revised model (Figure 4.18, with the model fit shown in Figure 4.19) is 105.600, with 26 degrees of freedom. The difference between them is 55.036, with a difference of 2 degrees of freedom. This value can then be compared with the chi-square distribution – a standard statistical distribution that is stored in most statistical software, and where tables of values are printed in many books. To get the result of this test, for example, you could open a Microsoft Excel file, and type into any cell:

$$= CHIDIST(50.036, 2)$$

The resulting value (approximating to zero) tells us that the p-value for this test is very small – certainly below 0.0001. Therefore we would reject the null hypothesis that there is no difference between the models, and choose the one with the better fit (the original, three factor model as shown in Figure 4.14).

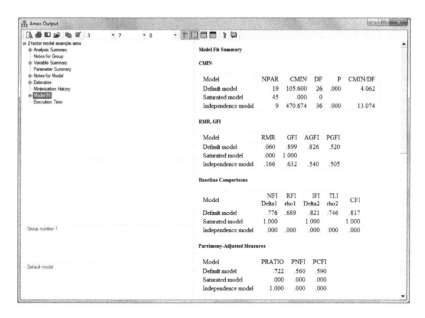

Figure 4.19 Fit of alternative model for personality items

Reprint Courtesy of International Business Machines Corporation, © International Business Machines Corporation

Once you have checked the fit of the most likely models (factor structures) that might underlie your data, you should be able to choose the best one, and proceed with the scales suggested by this for the rest of your analysis.

4.4.5 CFA: summary

As a reminder, if you are using CFA to confirm a factor structure, you should undertake the following steps:

1. Specify the main, hypothesized model clearly, and also any competing models that might be of interest.
2. For each of these, draw the model using the steps shown in section 4.4.2.
3. Run the model and examine the output, paying particular attention to the key measures of model fit, and the factor loadings of items.
4. If appropriate, do the same for competing models, comparing the fit. If one model is nested within another, use the chi-square test to compare them formally.
5. If your preferred model has two or more factors that are highly correlated, conduct the discriminant validity test to examine whether the factors can be reliably distinguished.

To read more about conducting CFA using Amos, I recommend reading the book by Byrne (2013).

4.5 RELIABILITY ANALYSIS

Checking the reliability of a set of items is considerably simpler than the factor analysis described in the previous sections!

In recent versions of SPSS, reliability analysis can be found by going to 'Analyze' > 'Scale' > 'Reliability Analysis'. Here, you can choose the items from a single scale (whether determined before starting the research, or suggested by factor analysis), and then in the 'Statistics' button, check the three boxes in the upper left-hand corner (see Figure 4.20 for an example).

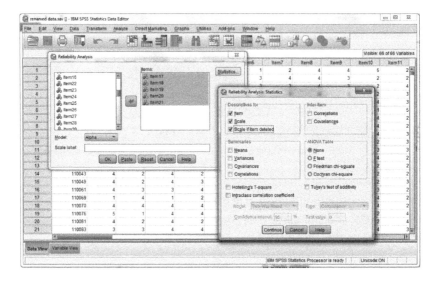

Figure 4.20   Specifying reliability analysis in SPSS

Reprint Courtesy of International Business Machines Corporation, © International Business Machines Corporation

Running this analysis will produce two key parts of the output. The first, and most important part, is the reliability itself, given by Cronbach's alpha. In the example in Figure 4.21, it can be seen that this is 0.915 – clearly above the 0.7 or 0.8 level considered acceptable, and therefore we would feel confident proceeding with this scale (see Chapter 6 for a discussion of whether 0.7 or 0.8 is more appropriate as a cut-off here).

However, the other table can also be of use at times. This gives us information about what would happen if any particular item were excluded from the scale. The final column 'Cronbach's Alpha if Item Deleted' tells us what the reliability would be if any one item were to be excluded. If one of these is very much higher than the Cronbach's alpha actually found, it suggests the item may not belong as part of that scale. This is most useful to know if the reliability is poor, and you are seeking to

Reliability Statistics

Cronbach's Alpha	N of Items
.915	5

Item-Total Statistics

	Scale Mean if Item Deleted	Scale Variance if Item Deleted	Corrected Item-Total Correlation	Cronbach's Alpha if Item Deleted
Item17	14.56	14.085	.797	.894
Item18	14.58	13.545	.837	.885
Item19	14.88	13.433	.794	.894
Item20	14.95	13.119	.768	.901
Item21	14.45	14.470	.731	.906

Figure 4.21 Reliability output in SPSS

Reprint Courtesy of International Business Machines Corporation, © International Business Machines Corporation

improve it – if the reliability is already above 0.8, the it is unlikely that you would want to exclude any items from the analysis.

The column before that, Corrected Item-Total Correlation, shows the correlation between each item and the scale that is formed by the rest of the items. If this is particularly low, it might suggest again that the item does not really belong as part of the scale, but is measuring something different. If this is negative, then it may suggest that the item needs reverse coding – the technique described in Chapter 3 (Box 3.3). If necessary, you can make the changes to the items/scale and calculate the reliability again.

Box 4.2   Composite reliability

As well as Cronbach's alpha, other methods can be used to measure reliability, some of which were explained in Chapter 2. One that was not, however, is 'Composite reliability', which is calculated from the output of confirmatory factor analysis, and estimates the reliability of the latent factors rather than of a straightforward mean (or total) score, as Cronbach's alpha does.

The calculation of composite reliability is not dissimilar from the methods used to check discriminant validity. Specifically, it is calculated by dividing the sum of the squared factor loadings (the same as the AVE multiplied by the number of items), by the total variance, which is the sum of the squared factor loadings *plus* the sum of variances of all of the error terms.

4.6 FURTHER ANALYSIS TECHNIQUES

Once the factor analysis and reliability analysis have been completed, you would calculate overall scale scores for each factor (using the technique described in Chapter 3, Box 3.6) and proceed with your subsequent analysis – e.g. descriptive analysis, hypothesis testing – using these. Box 3.5 gave a summary of some of the more common methods.

  These methods are not specific to survey data, and therefore are covered in many other texts. In particular, many are described in much more detail in the volume by Scherbaum and Shockley (2015).

4.7 CHAPTER SUMMARY

In this chapter we have mainly concentrated on three methods that are important in the processing of survey data based on scales (using classical test theory) – two types of factor analysis, exploratory and confirmatory, and reliability analysis. The two types of factor analysis are relatively complex, and whole books have been written about each. What is covered within this chapter is the basic methods and decision points that would apply to most management students using Likert-type scales from surveys. It is not intended to be a fully comprehensive manual for these techniques, but instead gives a guide that many students and researchers will be able to follow to apply to the majority of such situations.

CHAPTER REFERENCES

Byrne, B.M. (2013) *Structural Equation Modeling with Amos: Basic Concepts, Applications, and Programming* (2nd edn). New York: Routledge.

Conway, J.M. and Huffcutt, A.I. (2003) A review and evaluation of exploratory factor analysis practices in organizational research. *Organizational Research Methods*, 6, 147–168.

Fornell, C. and Larcker, D.F. (1981) Evaluating structural equation models with unobserved variables and measurement error. *Journal of Marketing Research*, 18, 39–50.

Scherbaum, C. and Shockley, K. (2015) *Analysing Quantitative Data for Business and Management Students*. London: Sage.

Thompson, B. and Daniel, L.G. (1996) Factor analytic evidence for the construct validity of scores: a historical overview and some guidelines. *Educational and Psychological Measurement*, 56(2), 197–208.

5

EXAMPLES OF ANALYSIS USING
CLASSICAL TEST THEORY

5.1 CHAPTER OVERVIEW

In the previous chapters we have seen an introduction to the principles of questionnaire data analysis using classical test theory, descriptions of the methodological assumptions, reliability and validity, and descriptions of how this analysis can be conducted (first by examining the components of such analysis, and then a more detailed description of the methods themselves). In this chapter we look at some examples of how these methods have been used in the management literature.

We describe three examples (sections 5.2 to 5.4) looking at separate papers, which involve key methods described in Chapter 4 - exploratory factor analysis, confirmatory factor analysis and reliability analysis. In each of these cases, the analysis itself forms part of a broader study, so we examine not just the use of classical test theory itself, but how it contributed to the overall aims of the study.

5.2 AN EXAMPLE OF EXPLORATORY FACTOR ANALYSIS

The example in this section comes from Parker (2007). This paper used two studies to investigate the links between employees' role orientation (the way individuals define their role) and different levels of job performance. In the first study, the author wanted to examine the effect of role orientation after controlling for three other factors that are known to predict performance: generalized self-efficacy (people's belief in their ability to do things well), internal locus of control (the expectation that the individual is able to control outcomes), and job aspiration (the extent to which an individual engages with their work environment beyond basic levels). She measured these three variables using new versions of scales, two of which were based on previous scales but were not identical, and one of which (internal locus of control) was entirely new. There were 11 items in total for these three factors.

Because of the stage of development of these scales – some of the items (questions) were new, and the set of items had not been used together in a study before – the author decided that an exploratory factor analysis (EFA) would be desirable. This was important because there may be correlations between these three factors: for example, someone with high job aspiration is also likely to have high self-efficacy, and so on. She therefore used an EFA to determine the factors. Figure 5.1 shows the table from her paper that gave the results of the factor loadings.

	Generalized self-efficacy	Internal locus of control	Job aspiration
I am good at thinking of better ways to do things	.73		
I am good at solving problems to do with work	.63		
I can do just about anything when I set my mind to it	.56		
People tend to come to me if they need help with work problems	.41		
When I make plans, I'm almost certain I can make them work	.35		
I feel in control of the way my life is going		.73	
What happens to me in the future mostly depends on my own efforts		.71	
I try to avoid added responsibilities in my job (rs)			.63
I am uneasy when faced with problems that have no single solution (rs)			.57
I enjoy the challenge of difficult targets			.50
I work hard to be the best at work I do			.34

Note: (rs) means the item was reversed scored. Factor loading < .30 not shown.

© SAGE Publications 2007. Reprinted with kind permission of SAGE Publications Ltd.

Figure 5.1 Results from an exploratory factor analysis of generalized self-efficacy, internal locus of control, and job aspiration items in Parker (2007: Table A, p. 432)

As is often the case in applied research, decisions about the different options in EFA are not clear-cut. Following best practice, Parker used principal axis factoring to extract the factors – this is particularly appropriate because of the expectation that there are separate constructs underlying the specific items. On the other hand, she chose to use a Varimax (orthogonal) rotation rather than an oblique rotation such as Direct Oblimin. This she justified on the basis that the three underlying constructs were supposed to be different theoretically, and it was desirable to capture the non-overlapping elements of these. However, the three factors are still expected to be correlated, so many would argue that an oblique rotation would be preferable. In reality, though, it may not make a difference to the result achieved.

The three factors extracted all had eigenvalues greater than 1. Parker did not state exactly what these eigenvalues were, or show a scree plot (or conduct parallel analysis), so we are left assume that this was the correct number of factors. In this circumstance, given the number of factors with eigenvalues above one fitted the expected solution, this was probably a non-controversial decision, and such information is often left out of papers if there is pressure on the space available (e.g. if the target word count is approached or exceeded). However, if there is any doubt about the number of factors, then the decision should be justified to readers.

The table shown in Figure 5.1 gives the factor loadings, omitting those below 0.3 as suggested in Chapter 4. The remaining factor loadings are relatively clear in terms of which item belongs to which factor – there are no cross-loadings, and all items load on one of the three. However, note that two of the item loadings are lower than might be desirable (0.34 and 0.35). In a different situation, where there was a less clear prior belief about which items would be part of which factors, this might be enough reason to exclude these items. However, given the prior expectation, the author opted to keep all items in the analysis. This is maybe something that contributed to lower values of Cronbach's alpha than would be expected (between 0.67 and 0.74).

Indeed, it may be that because of the strength of the prior expectation about which items would load on which factors a confirmatory factor analysis would be more appropriate in this instance. The decision between EFA and CFA is something that was covered in Chapter 3; as this example shows, the process for making this decision is not always clear-cut.

Parker (2007) subsequently uses these scales to show that there is indeed a relationship between role orientation and job performance (both four months ahead, and 18 months ahead), even after taking into account the effects of generalized self-efficacy, locus of control and job aspiration. Therefore the EFA used to demonstrate the separate nature of each of these scales was of critical importance in delineating the contribution that this study made to the literature. In a second study within the same paper, she demonstrated that this effect is moderated by the level of job autonomy that employees have: this second study also includes two examples of EFA (the first on items comprising scales for job satisfaction, role orientation, job aspiration and generalized self-efficacy; the second on items relating to company performance), and these are conducted and reported in a similar way to the EFA from the first study. Although this analysis is not repeated here, it provides another set of examples for readers to examine in the original paper should they wish.

5.3 AN EXAMPLE OF CONFIRMATORY FACTOR ANALYSIS

The example in this section comes from Daniels (2000). In this paper, he aims to provide evidence of validity for five aspects of affective well-being in the work context (in other words, how happy and mentally healthy employees are at work). These five aspects are not labelled by single names, but instead each gives opposite ends of a continuum along which an individual would fall, these being abbreviated to two letters: anxiety–comfort (AC); depression–pleasure (DP); bored–enthusiastic (BE); tiredness–vigour (TV); and angry–placid (AP).

Specifically, using two large samples (the first with 871 respondents, the second with 1,915) the author compares four possible hypothesized models that would account for how the 30 items are grouped into factors (each item being a word or short phrase to which the respondent would indicate the extent to which it applied to them, e.g. cheerful, aggressive, full of energy). Importantly, the models that were compared were all based on theoretical arguments arising from relevant literature. The depression–pleasure items were the same in all four models; models 1 and 2 both had six items per factor, but differed in that one of the anxiety–comfort items ('calm') and one of the angry–placid items ('at ease') swapped between the models. In models 3 and 4 two of the tiredness–vigour items ('alert' and 'full of energy') became bored–enthusiastic items instead, but otherwise the items were as per models 1 and 2 respectively.

The two samples were of social services workers and university workers respectively. The first study also collected data on job characteristics, job competence, and positive and negative affectivity (general positive and negative feelings); the second collected data on general health via the SF-36 (a standardized measure of health comprising 36 items across nine dimensions; Ware and Sherbourne, 1992) to help demonstrate the criterion-related validity. The CFA was conducted across both samples simultaneously, using a feature that forces the same model (including the same factor loadings) to be used in both samples.

As well as comparing the four models described above, Daniels compared other models in which there were fewer than five factors by combining factors in different ways. This is made clear in Figure 5.2, which also shows the results of the analysis. In addition to these models, he also examined a 'second order' model, in which all of the factors identified are hypothesized as parts of a single, larger factor, explaining well-being generally.

The table shown in Figure 5.2 includes a variety of statistics about each model – some of which are more useful than others. The chi-square (χ^2) statistic, and associated degrees of freedom and p-value, are useful for certain types of model comparison but do not present a good measure of absolute model fit. The AIC and CAIC refer to Akaike's Information Criterion and the Consistent Akaike's Information Criterion – these are measures that adjust the level of fit according to the complexity of the model, and therefore can be used to compare models that are not nested. The AIC imposes a 'penalty' on a model when it is more complex (i.e. decreases the model fit if there is more complexity in the model); the CAIC imposes an even stricter penalty. The smaller the value of these indices, the better the model fit. The NFI (Normed Fit Index) is another fit index that is sometimes used, but can be biased by sample size so is not universally considered helpful. The NNF (Non-Normed Fit) is another term for the Tucker-Lewis Index, described in Chapter 4, and the Comparative Fit Index was also described in Chapter 4. It is these indices - alongside the AIC/CAIC - that give the best indication of model fit in this situation (although some pairs of models can be directly compared using a chi-square difference test too).

It appears that the best fitting model is model 2 in the second row. This is because it has the highest NNF (TLI) and CFI (.91 and .92 respectively), and the lowest AIC (and CAIC) (3412.87 and –1839.48 respectively). The second order model (bottom row of the table) is close to this; all others are clearly worse.

In particular, the 'Other primary factor' models use two, three or four factors overall (with factors grouped as shown in the brackets - so in model (d), AC and AP belong to a single factor, and DP and BE belong to another single factor). These all have clearly inferior fit than models 1-4, which all have five factors. If, for example, we wanted to

Model	χ^2	df	p<	AIC	CAIC	NFI	NNF	CFI
1	5174.21	770	.001	3634.21	−1618.15	.90	.90	.91
2	4952.87	770	.001	3412.87	−1839.48	.90	.91	.92
3*	5327.80	770	.001	3787.80	−1464.55	.89	.90	.91
4*	5111.01	770	.001	3571.01	−1681.35	.90	.90	.91
Other primary factor models** 2 factors								
(a) (AC DP AP)(BE TV)	6524.15	779	.001	4966.15	−347.60	.87	.87	.88
(b) (AC AP DP)(DP AP TV)	5893.77	773	.001	4347.77	24.18	.88	.88	.90
(c) (AC AP) (DP BE TV)	6895.93	779	.001	5337.93	−925.05	.86	.86	.88
3 factors								
(d) (AC AP) (DP BE) (TV)	6505.42	777	.001	4951.42	−348.68	.87	.87	.88
(e) (AC AP) (DP) (BE TV)	5841.10	777	.001	4287.10	−1013.01	.88	.87	.90
(f) (AC DP) (AP) (BE TV)	5819.15	777	.001	4265.15	−1034.95	.89	.89	.90
4 factors								
(g) (AC AP) (DP) (BE) (TV)	5396.37	774	.001	3848.37	−1431.28	.89	.89	.90
(h) (AC DP) (AP) (BE) (TV)	5757.76	774	.001	4209.76	−1069.88	.89	.89	.90
(i) (AP) (AC) (DP BE) (TV)	5862.59	774	.001	4314.59	−965.05	.88	.89	.90
(j) (AC) (AP) (DP) (BE TV)	5595.59	774	.001	4047.58	−1232.06	.89	.89	.90
2nd order model	5021.20	800	.001	3421.20	−2035.80	.90	.91	.92

© SAGE Publications 2000. Reprinted with kind permission of SAGE Publications Ltd.

Figure 5.2 Example of confirmatory factor analysis: goodness of fit statistics for different models of well-being items in Daniels (2000: Table 2, p. 284))

compare model (g) with model 2, we can do this using a formal test because the two models are nested (model (g) is effectively the same as model 2 but with two of the factors having a correlation of 1, i.e. being the same). The difference in chi-square is 443.5 (with a difference of 4 degrees of freedom); consulting a table of chi-square statistics or plugging this into a chi-square calculator will tell us that the models are significantly different, $p < .001$. Therefore we can conclude that the model with the lower chi-square (model 2) is significantly better at fitting to the data.

Box 5.1   Which fit indices should you display?

Different authors will show different selections of fit indices. This reflects both the changing understanding of which fit indices are the most appropriate indices over time (CFA is still a relatively new procedure compared with many other statistical methods), and also that there are subtle differences in situations that may require some indices to be favoured above others. In general it is a good idea to follow the example of a relevant (comparable) recent article in a reputable journal, or otherwise to stick with the indices suggested in Chapter 4 (CFI, TLI, RMSEA and SRMR in particular).

The paper then goes on to show the factor loadings (column heading FL) for model 2: these are shown in Figure 5.3.

The standard errors (column heading SE) are also shown here, indicating that all loadings are statistically significant, as $p < .05$ for all. What is more relevant, however, is that most of the loadings are high, with only two being a bit lower – notably the item 'fatigued'. In an exploratory procedure, this might lead us to omit this item from future analysis; in a CFA, however, it is usually the case that (unless the fit is unacceptably low) all the items would be retained as hypothesized. Therefore the paper proceeds with all items included.

Note also that some of the loadings are positive and some negative: this reflects the fact that some of the items relate to positive states of well-being, and some relate to negative states (this is similar to the positively and negatively worded statements that are often used as Likert scale items and sometimes need recoding before further analysis, as discussed in section 3.2). Interestingly, it is the positive well-being items that have the negative loadings (e.g. in the AC factor, 'anxious' has a positive loading, 0.83, but 'at ease' has a negative loading, −0.66): this simply reflects the particular mathematics underlying the procedure, and nothing untoward can be read into it. It does suggest, however, that, if the latent variables were to be used in further analysis, a higher score would relate to a lower level of well-being (which would be important to recognize in the interpretation of these results).

	A–C		D–P		B–E		T–V		A–P	
Item	FL	SE	FL	SE	FL	SE	FL	SE	FL	SE
Anxious	.83	.03								
Worried	.78	.04								
Tense	.77	.02								
At ease	−.66	.03								
Relaxed	−.57	.02								
Comfortable	−.54	.02								
Depressed			.80	.02						
Miserable			.76	.02						
Gloomy			.85	.02						
Happy			−.65	.02						
Pleased			−.50	.02						
Cheerful			−.59	.02						
Bored					.69	.02				
Sluggish					.59	.02				
Dull					.76	.02				
Enthusiastic					−.81	.02				
Optimistic					−.59	.02				
Motivated					−.82	.02				
Tired							−.69	.02		
Fatigued							.59	.02		
Sleepy							.76	.02		
Active							−.81	.02		
Alert							−.59	.02		
Full of energy							−.82	.02		
Angry									.87	.02
Annoyed									.79	.02
Aggressive									.67	.02
Placid									−.35	.03
Patient									−.44	.03
Calm									−.50	.02

Key: FL = factor loading, SE = standard error

All loadings, $p < .001$

Loadings on response bias factors were not constrained to be equal in both samples. For clarity, these loadings are omitted. They are available from the author on request.

© SAGE Publications 2000. Reprinted with kind permission of SAGE Publications Ltd.

Figure 5.3   CFA item factor loadings and standard errors, in Daniels (2000: Table 3, p. 285)

Daniels (2000) does go on to look at the link between these five factors and the other measures collected, although using partial correlations (not using the latent variables, which would have required a structural equation modelling approach). He finds that there are several significant correlations even controlling for all other well-being variables: for example, in the university worker sample tiredness–vigour is correlated with energy at 0.50 ($p < .001$), and bored–enthusiastic is correlated with under–overload at 0.41 ($p < .001$). Indeed, each factor has at least one correlation with an expected other variable with $p < .001$. This therefore presents strong criterion-related validity for the measure, as well as the construct-related validity provided by the CFA. These are two elements of the scale development process that we will see again in the example in section 5.4.

5.4 AN EXAMPLE OF RELIABILITY ANALYSIS

The example in this section comes from Kravitz, Bludau and Klineberg (2008). This paper examines factors linked to attitudes towards affirmative action in organizations (procedures aimed at eliminating discrimination and enhancing opportunities for employees from minority groups). It presented two studies, with the second study using four measures for which reliability was measured via Cronbach's alpha, but also a single-item measure as the dependent variable for which Cronbach's alpha cannot be calculated, as the formula relies on having multiple items.

There were four scales in the questionnaire that was used by the authors: anticipated impact of the affirmative action plan (AAP) on the respondents' personal and collective self-interest (five items); the anticipated impact of AAP on representation of the target group (eight items); anticipate impact of AAP on stigmatization of the target group (seven items); and anticipated impact of AAP on company performance (eight items). Reliability analysis showed these had Cronbach's alphas of 0.89, 0.65, 0.76 and 0.85 respectively. Interestingly, the authors described the reliability of 0.65 as 'minimally acceptable', suggesting that this is high enough to be considered as having an adequate absence of measurement error. This would be disputed by some, as will be discussed in Chapter 6.

Another interesting feature of the reliability analysis in this study, however, is the use of a single-item measure for the dependent variable,[1] the attitude towards AAPs. Single-item measures are often discouraged for a variety of reasons, the most important being that they often lack validity. However, occasionally there is no realistic alternative, and another problem with single-item measures is that Cronbach's alpha cannot be calculated – as the formula relies on having multiple items. Kravitz and colleagues get round this problem in an ingenious way: by using the measure on the same sample twice (approximately a month apart), and using test–retest reliability.

---

[1] The first study also uses single-item measures for some of the independent variables: this limitation is addressed by using multi-item scales in study 2.

This gave a value of 0.85, providing strong evidence for a relative lack of measurement error, and suggesting that the measure used is reliable.

This gives additional credence to the authors' ultimate findings that there was a positive relationship between anticipated impacts of AAP and support for the AAP, but that the strength of this relationship differed between racial groups: in general, the relationships were strongest among White employees.

5.5 CHAPTER SUMMARY

In this chapter we have looked at three examples of how different statistical procedures for analysing quantitative survey data have been used within the context of three different, wider studies. One of these studies – Daniels (2000) – was primarily about proving validity of the scales in question, and showed how alternative models can be tested within such a study. The other two studies were based on more substantive research questions about the relationships between different constructs, and the methods shown (exploratory factor analysis in Parker, 2007, and different forms of reliability analysis in Kravitz et al., 2008) are really the means to an end: without the support for reliability and validity shown by these methods, the authors would not be able to make the claims they do about the contribution their study is making to the wider literature.

There are countless other examples that could have been chosen. Almost all studies using multi-item scales will at least report a form of reliability – usually internal consistency, as measured by Cronbach's alpha. Many will also report either an EFA or a CFA, or occasionally both. Some articles that are primarily about scale development will show all of these (and sometimes more) within a single paper. Others will use methods in slightly different ways: for example, Patterson et al. (2005) involves the development of an 82-item, 17-dimension questionnaire to measure organizational climate, and collects a large sample, which is split randomly into two (as described in Chapter 3). However, rather than using EFA on the first sub-sample, they use CFA to refine the theoretically derived hypothesized structure of the items, and then test this using the second sub-sample.

CFA can also be used as a step towards conducting structural equation modelling (which is a way of examining relationships between latent variables, often measured via questionnaire items). For example, Korschun, Bhattacharya and Swain (2014) developed a model linking organization and customer views on corporate social responsibility, company identification and organizational customer orientation and performance (a total of seven constructs). Before using a structural equation model to test their hypotheses, they used CFA to examine the 'measurement model' – a factor model where all latent variables are correlated (compared with the structural equation model, where some variables are not directly linked with each other). Among other fit indices they reported a CFI of 0.94, an RMSEA of 0.05 and an SRMR of 0.05 – all of which support their model linking specific items to specific constructs. They were then able to use this data to test their five hypotheses (four of which were supported) using structural equation modelling.

Some studies in the field of management will use these methods for data that are not in the same form (i.e. not collected via Likert-type scales). For example, Erkens and Bonner (2012) use principal components analysis to construct a measure of 'Firm status' that includes three measures: a firm's market capitalization, the number of firms with which a firm is connected through common board members, and the Fortune Most Admired Companies rating. Note that, as these are not measures constructed using classical test theory, the choice of principal components analysis as opposed to conventional EFA is justified, and the authors found that a single component explained a sufficient amount of the variability (nearly 60%) in all three items.

Which precise methods a project or paper will need to utilize (and report on) will depend on the precise scope and objectives of the study – see Chapter 3 for more on this decision-making procedure. However, the examples provided in this chapter give a good demonstration of how they can be incorporated into the writing up of a wider study. They also illustrate some of the debates that surround the methods in this book – these will be described further in Chapter 6.

CHAPTER REFERENCES

Daniels, K. (2000) Measures of five aspects of affective well-being at work. *Human Relations*, 53(2), 275-294.

Erkens, D.H. and Bonner, S.E. (2012) The role of firm status in appointments of accounting financial experts to audit committees. *The Accounting Review*, 88(1), 107-136.

Korschun, D., Bhattacharya, C.B. and Swain, S.D. (2014) Corporate social responsibility, customer orientation, and the job performance of frontline employees. *Journal of Marketing*, 78(3), 20-37.

Kravitz, D.A., Bludau, T.M. and Klineberg, S.L. (2008) The impact of anticipated consequences, respondent group, and strength of affirmative action plan on affirmative action attitudes. *Group and Organization Management*, 33(4), 361-391.

Parker, S.K. (2007) 'That is my job': how employees' role orientation affects their job performance. *Human Relations*, 60(3), 403-434.

Patterson, M.G., West, M.A., Shackleton, V.J., Dawson, J.F., Lawthom, R., Maitlis, S., Robinson, D.L. and Wallace, A.M. (2005) Validating the organizational climate measure: links to managerial practices, productivity and innovation. *Journal of Organizational Behavior*, 26, 379-408.

Ware Jr, J.E. and Sherbourne, C.D. (1992) The MOS 36-item short-form health survey (SF-36): I. Conceptual framework and item selection. *Medical Care*, 30, 473-483.

6

CONCLUSIONS

6.1 CHAPTER OVERVIEW

In the previous chapters we have seen the basis of classical test theory and the statistical methods used to analyse quantitative survey data – particularly data gathered using multi-item scales. At various stages, these chapters have hinted at assumptions that need to be made, or decisions that might not be obvious. This chapter examines a few of the key issues in analysis of multi-item scales that have sometimes proved controversial: what constitutes acceptable reliability; what exploratory factor analysis options should be used; whether exploratory or confirmatory factor analyses are more appropriate; and what software should be used for confirmatory factor analysis. The chapter finishes with a recap of the steps that need to be undertaken, and the decisions to be made during the process. However, first we take a step back and consider whether classical test theory is the most appropriate paradigm to use at all.

6.2 CLASSICAL TEST THEORY COMPARED WITH OTHER PARADIGMS

As we have seen throughout the earlier chapters, classical test theory is commonly used in analysis of quantitative survey data, and its popularity can be put down to a combination of the simplicity of the underlying model, and the fact that often it provides a very good method of retrieving data about something that cannot be measured directly. However, there are some valid criticisms of CTT that are worth considering. We will examine two of these concerns here, and describe alternative models that attempt to address these.

The first concern is that CTT assumes there is an underlying, latent variable that underpins the responses to all items. This is the central idea behind CTT, and relies on the idea that all respondents will have their own value of the underlying construct, and that this will be reflected in the way they respond to the relevant items. For this reason, the method of measurement is sometimes referred to as 'reflective' measurement.

However, there are other models that could also explain the relationship between a set of items and a construct. One that has been gaining some popularity in recent years is what is called 'formative' measurement – one in which the items do not reflect an underlying construct, but that the construct itself is formed out of the responses to different items. For example, a measure of a company's proactive market orientation may be formed by measuring the different proactive strategies used summing these up; there is no reason to believe that a company with a moderately proactive orientation would have moderate scores on all of the different strategies, as they may employ some but not others: therefore there would be little or no internal consistency in a scale formed in this way.

Although this appears an attractive way to measure some constructs where a traditional CTT approach would be more difficult, it is fraught with limitations. Many of these are explained in detail by Edwards (2011). In particular, the reliability and validity of measures cannot be assessed in the usual way, and so there is less certainty about the validity of findings. It is more important that the exact formation of measures (i.e. which items are included) is theoretically correct, as the addition or removal of a single item is likely to have a larger effect on scores than a measure constructed using CTT. It is also more difficult to analyse the data in a way that deals with many of these concerns.

The second concern is the underlying assumption that two individuals, with the same value of the latent variable (e.g. if the construct being measured is extraversion, then two individuals who are equally extravert) will respond to the same item in the same way (excluding measurement error). This is a fundamental assumption of CTT, and without it, the calculation of an overall score for a construct (e.g. extraversion) by the simple calculation of the mean of a set of items, does not apply. However, it is entirely reasonable, in some circumstances, to believe that different individuals may respond in a slightly different way to the same item, even if they do have the same underlying value of the construct being examined. For example, one individual may be generally more positive than another, and therefore be more likely to answer 'agree' or 'strongly agree' to the item 'I see myself as someone who is talkative', despite both individuals being as talkative as each other.

This limitation of CTT is addressed in a different paradigm for the interpretation and analysis of questionnaire items: item response theory (IRT). IRT uses a more complex model of how people respond to items, which differs from CTT principally in two ways. First, it does not assume that the ordinal response scale is actually an approximation of the underlying latent variable (so, for example, the difference between 'strongly disagree' and 'disagree' may be different from the difference between 'agree' and 'strongly agree' in terms of how big a difference in the underlying construct this is; moreover, this is not necessarily the same from one item to the next). Second, it introduces a 'person parameter' – an element of the model that accounts for differences between individuals' style in answering questions.

In many ways this produces a greatly more advanced, more sophisticated model of responses to items, which in turn allows a more precise estimation of the constructs in question. While this is a good thing, there are several disadvantages:

- The amount of data required is substantially larger: to estimate scores accurately some authors suggest that a sample of at least 500 is needed.
- It is not possible to conduct IRT in most standard software, such as SPSS; instead, specialist software such as PARSCALE or WinGen would be required.
- The interpretation of models is more complex, meaning that simple conclusions about effects are less easy to disentangle.

As a result, for most simple studies, CTT would remain the preferred option – unless there is evidence to suggest that a particular construct demands IRT, and there is a lot of data available (or that could be gathered). If this is the case, then it is advised that the reader consults a more comprehensive text about IRT, such as Embretson and Reise (2000).

6.3 DIFFERENT VIEWS ON RELIABILITY

One of the most common debates about quantitative survey data in the management literature is about what constitutes acceptable reliability of a multi-item scale. For many years it was regularly cited in the literature that 0.70 or higher would be sufficiently high to represent adequate reliability. Very often authors would refer to Nunnally's (1978) book on psychometric theory as a source for this. However, Lance, Butts and Michels (2006) reviewed the literature carefully, and found that in most cases this was based on a misreading of Nunnally's work – or, in reality, authors citing other authors (often citing other authors still, and so on) who had provided this misinterpretation.

What Nunnally (1978) actually said was that 0.70 would be the minimum required level of reliability even to entertain the notion of continuing to develop a scale, but for applied research a reliability of at least 0.80 would be needed. The reasons for this are that there is so much measurement error involved – even with a reliability of 0.80, a fifth of the variation in a score can be put down to error – that with reliabilities below 0.80, there is little cause to believe that an individual score will be very accurate. Therefore it is recommended that, if a cut-off for acceptable reliability is to be applied, this is 0.80 rather than 0.70.

Some authors would argue that measuring internal consistency is not the most important feature of reliability, and that test-retest reliability is actually more important, as this demonstrates the stability of a measure. Certainly for some measurements, where multi-item scales are not used, this gives a good way of checking a form of reliability (as demonstrated via the example in section 5.4). I would agree test-retest reliability is useful where it is possible to measure it, but for multi-item scales I would suggest that internal consistency (as measured via Cronbach's alpha) is always calculated also.

6.4 EXPLORATORY FACTOR ANALYSIS AND PRINCIPAL COMPONENTS ANALYSIS

Exploratory factor analysis (EFA) is very similar to a different procedure, principal components analysis (PCA). Both methods start with a set of variables (items), and examine the covariances or correlations between the items to discover groupings of variables. The difference between the methods is that EFA excludes variance that is unique to single variables – that is, it only takes into account the variation in items that is shared with variation in other items. In contrast PCA looks at all of the variation in all of the variables. Mathematically the difference is that the correlation matrix being analysed would have '1' down the diagonal in the PCA, but would have the communalities down the diagonal in the EFA.

There is an important difference in the rationale for the two methods. PCA is generally used as a method of data reduction – a procedure to convert a large number of variables into a smaller number of variables, but without any prior idea that the variables are based on a set of underlying constructs. It takes a purely exploratory approach, and is entirely open to the idea that variables may be unrelated to anything else. On the other hand, EFA is specifically based on the factor model – the classical test theory model described throughout this book. It assumes that the responses to items are composed of a factor score, plus some (random) error. Therefore ignoring an item's unique variance is a way of ignoring this error. For this reason EFA is the preferred approach any time there is reason to believe that the responses to items are based on underlying constructs (latent variables) – i.e. when using multi-item scales.

The two methods are often confused, however, and this is not helped by the fact that in SPSS the default method of 'factor analysis' is actually PCA! It is important to specify the correct method under the 'Extraction' button when performing EFA in SPSS - this would normally be principal axis factoring, as this is the method that corresponds to classical test theory most closely (although maximum likelihood has some additional advantages when the data are normally distributed).

It is essential, however, to consider whether EFA or PCA is the correct method for your analysis. In line with the recommendations of several authors, however, including Conway and Huffcutt (2003), I recommend that EFA is used for quantitative survey data, at least where the items are Likert-type scales.

Whether EFA or PCA is used, there is still a decision to be made about the type of rotation to be used for the solution – particularly whether it is an orthogonal or oblique rotation. This distinction was explained in section 4.2.4, and so is not repeated here, other than to reiterate the advice that oblique rotations are more appropriate whenever a correlation between factors is expected – which is normally the case in survey data.

Some authors have suggested that an orthogonal rotation (such as Varimax) is more likely to result in what is known as 'simple structure'; that is, a factor structure that cleanly separates items into separate factors more easily. However, Bandalos and Boehm-Kaufman (2009) examine this claim and conclude that such arguments only hold when there is sufficient distinction between factors in the first place: that is, whenever there is reason to believe that the underlying factors would be non-trivially correlated, an oblique rotation is better.

Despite these arguments, it is worth noting that in many cases the choice between EFA and PCA, and the choice between orthogonal and oblique rotations, makes little difference to the results, and very often the same conclusions are reached (Thompson, 2004). However, in some circumstances the results will differ, and it is in these instances that making the correct decision becomes important.

6.5 EXPLORATORY VERSUS CONFIRMATORY FACTOR ANALYSIS

As discussed in previous chapters, there are two different forms of factor analysis: exploratory factor analysis and confirmatory factor analysis. As suggested by their names, EFA is a predominantly exploratory procedure, used when there is uncertainty about which items should be part of which scales. CFA is used to confirm whether a hypothesized factor structure (the way items belong to certain scales) is supported by the data.

In some cases, the choice between EFA and CFA is clear. In the early stages of scale development, or if a set of items has been brought together without much thought to the underlying constructs, then EFA is certainly more appropriate. It is also appropriate in determining whether a set of items is based on one construct or more than one. On the other hand, CFA can be used directly whenever a set of existing items from a group of scales, which have been validated in previous studies, is used. However, in between these opposite ends of the spectrum there is room for some doubt.

For example, if an existing multi-item scale is used, but some items are altered slightly, or one or two new items added in, is it necessary to use EFA? Increasingly the prevailing opinion is that it would be better to proceed directly to CFA whenever a clearly hypothesized factor structure is argued (e.g. Levine et al., 2006). Even where the sample size permits the splitting of the sample into two sub-samples for exploratory and confirmatory procedures, if the factor structure is reasonably clear then it can be better to use CFA on both sub-samples: the first for model refinement (e.g. comparing models with different numbers of factors, deleting poor items), and the second for checking the goodness of fit of the model. The article by Patterson et al. (2005), previously mentioned in Chapter 5, gives a good example of how this might be used in practice.

The use of CFA, however, gives rise to another source of debate: which fit indices should be used. This has been a subject of much research itself over the last 25 years, with Hu and Bentler (1998) giving the first comprehensive review of indices available in structural equation modelling. For CFA specifically, Williams, Ford and Nguyen (2002) give useful advice that the Comparative Fit Index, Tucker-Lewis Index and Root Mean Squared Error of Approximation form a good set of indices to use; I would add to this list the Standardized Root Mean Square Residual as Hu and Bentler found this to be the best individual index.

It is worth bearing in mind, however, that the suggested cut-offs for these indices as quoted in Chapter 4 are themselves subject to debate (and that, as shown in Chapter 5, this manifests itself with different interpretations in the literature). More recently, Nye and Drasgow (2011) have argued that simple rules of thumb are not always appropriate, and in some fields of research, even relatively poor fit might be acceptable if it exceeds what has been found in that field previously. Therefore, when assessing whether a model fit is acceptable, it is important to consider what has been found for similar scales in similar settings in prior research.

6.6 SOFTWARE FOR CONDUCTING CONFIRMATORY FACTOR ANALYSIS

Most of the analytic methods covered in this book can be performed using the general statistical software SPSS, and the examples given have used SPSS to show how this can be done. Of course, most are also possible in any general, comprehensive statistical software programme. However, confirmatory factor analysis is not possible using SPSS, or some other standard statistical software, as it requires a structural equation modelling environment to run.

Therefore Table 6.1 shows some of the software options that can be used to run CFA, or other structural equation models.

Table 6.1 Software for conducting CFA

Software name	Notes
Amos	Distributed by SPSS, and therefore often available where SPSS is available – but not always. Has a graphical interface – the model is drawn – which makes it easy to use in one respect but fiddly in others. Not capable of running as sophisticated models as some software, but covers basic CFA very well. The examples in Chapter 4 of this book use Amos.
Mplus	Highly sophisticated structural equation modelling software, built to cope with multi-level models and other more complex data structures. Syntax-driven, but relatively easy to learn. However, only available in single user licences, and more expensive as a result.
LISREL	The original structural equation modelling software. Has developed well over the years and now has an optional graphical interface, as well as being able to deal with some of the more complex data structures that Mplus can as well.
EQS	Another specialist structural equation modelling software, also with a graphical interface and relatively easy to use.
Open Mx	Open-source (and free) structural equation modelling software that uses syntax to run models – not especially easy to use, but once learned can be very quick.
Stata	Comprehensive and highly rated general statistical software. CFA can be conducted via its structural equation modelling procedure. Not recommended if choosing a separate package for CFA, but Stata users do not need to use different software for this purpose.
SAS	Comprehensive and widely used general statistical software. CFA can be conducted via the CALIS procedure. Not recommended if choosing a separate package for CFA, but SAS users do not need to use different software for this purpose.
R	Comprehensive, free and open-source general statistical software. CFA can be conducted via different add-on packages. Entirely syntax driven and less easy to learn from scratch; therefore not recommended if choosing a separate package for CFA (unless cost is a priority and there is plenty of time to learn the syntax), but R users may wish to choose this option.

6.7 OVERVIEW OF ANALYSIS PROCEDURE AND DECISIONS WITH MULTI-ITEM SCALES

As covered in Chapter 3, there are several steps that should be undertaken when using multi-item scales. Now that we have covered each of these procedures and identified some of the decisions that need to be taken, it is timely to revisit this list of steps, and clarify what needs to be checked within each one.

1. Enter data into appropriate software

   Data should be entered carefully, checked and set up with full variable names and labels as appropriate for the software. The examples in this book are based around SPSS, but other statistical software (e.g. Stata, SAS) is just as possible.

2. Check and clean data

Descriptive statistical procedures are particularly useful here. Variables should be checked to ensure there are no impossible values, and where possible the reasons for missing data are known.

3. Factor analysis

First you need to decide whether exploratory or confirmatory factor analysis is needed, or both. If exploratory analysis is needed, decisions need to be taken about:

- the extraction method (usually recommended is principal axis factoring)
- the rotation method (usually recommended is Direct Oblimin)
- the number of factors to retain (this should be based, in part at least, on the scree plot)
- what minimum factor loadings are appropriate (usually 0.4 or 0.5 would be best).

If confirmatory analysis is needed, you will have to use software other than SPSS - in this book examples in Amos are given. You should also consider other models that might be plausible (e.g. with factors combined), and test these to compare fit. The model with the best overall fit statistics (e.g. CFI, TLI, SRMR, RMSEA) is usually chosen. If correlations between factors are high (greater than 0.5), you should also test for discriminant validity between these factors.

Note that you should never report exploratory and confirmatory factor analysis results based on the same data.

1. Recoding any oppositely scored items

A useful rule to check which items should be recoded is to examine the factor loadings for each factor, and if there is a mixture of positive and negative loadings among the items that are assigned to that factor, those with negative loadings (or, alternatively, those with positive loadings) should be recoded as described in section 3.2.

2. Check reliability

First determine whether Cronbach's alpha is the most appropriate form of reliability to use. In most cases it will be, but occasionally test-retest reliability might be feasible, or if using latent variables, composite reliability can be used instead. The reliability of each scale should ideally be at least 0.80. If it is between 0.70 and 0.80, then this may be considered acceptable but not ideal. If it is below 0.70, this would be a reason to amend the scale.

3. Amend scales (if necessary)

If the reliability is too low, then it might be possible to improve it by excluding one or more items that have particularly low factor loadings. If this does not succeed, then it may be necessary to go back to step 3, and choose factor analysis solutions based on slightly different criteria (e.g. fewer factors extracted from the exploratory factor analysis procedure).

4. Calculate overall scale scores

   Once adequate reliability – and, if needed, discriminant validity – has been demonstrated, overall scale scores can be calculated using the method described in section 3.5. These are then used in all subsequent analysis, rather than the individual items.

5. Analyse data using overall scale scores

   Data analysis proceeds with appropriate methods for the particular research question, as suggested in section 3.6. See Scherbaum and Shockley (2015) for more information on these methods.

6.8 CHAPTER SUMMARY

In this chapter we have examined some of the more complex decisions to be made when analysing quantitative survey data. In particular, we have considered whether classical test theory is appropriate, and if so, what precise methods should be used for data analysis. In doing so it has summarized some of the arguments and recommendations found in the wider literature about reliability analysis, exploratory factor analysis (compared with principal components analysis and with confirmatory factor analysis), and how confirmatory factor analysis can be conducted adequately.

Most of the issues discussed in this chapter are still 'hot' issues in the literature: even though some consensus may have emerged in recent years, there are still some authors who may disagree with the recommendations presented here. It is wise, therefore, to remember that although the recommendations in this chapter – and elsewhere in the book – may represent overall considerations about best practice, in specific situations there may be reasons to use other methods. In the absence of other advice, however, the suggestions here should probably be followed.

CHAPTER REFERENCES

Bandalos, D.L. and Boehm-Kaufman, M.R. (2009) Four common misconceptions in exploratory factor analysis. In C.E. Lance and R.J. Vandenberg (eds), *Statistical and Methodological Myths and Urban Legends: Doctrine, Verity and Fable in the Organizational and Social Sciences.* New York: Routledge, pp. 61–87.

Conway, J.M. and Huffcutt, A.I. (2003) A review and evaluation of exploratory factor analysis practices in organizational research. *Organizational Research Methods,* 6, 147–168.

Edwards, J.R. (2011) The fallacy of formative measurement. *Organizational Research Methods*, 14(2), 370-388.

Embretson, S. and Reise, S. (2000) *Item Response Theory for Psychologists*. Mahwah, NJ: Erlbaum.

Hu, L.T. and Bentler, P.M. (1998) Fit indices in covariance structure modeling: sensitivity to underparameterized model misspecification. *Psychological Methods*, 3, 424-453.

Lance, C.E., Butts, M.M. and Michels, L.C. (2006) The sources of four commonly reported cutoff criteria: what did they really say? *Organizational Research Methods*, 9(2), 202-220.

Levine, T., Hullett, C.R., Turner, M.M. and Lapinski, M.K. (2006) The desirability of using confirmatory factor analysis on published scales. *Communication Research Reports*, 23(4), 309-314.

Nunnally, J.C. (1978) *Psychometric Theory*. New York: McGraw Hill.

Nye, C.D. and Drasgow, F. (2011) Assessing goodness of fit: simple rules of thumb simply do not work. *Organizational Research Methods*, 14, 548-570.

Patterson, M.G., West, M.A., Shackleton, V.J., Dawson, J.F., Lawthom, R., Maitlis, S., Robinson, D.L. and Wallace, A.M. (2005) Validating the organizational climate measure: links to managerial practices, productivity and innovation. *Journal of Organizational Behavior*, 26, 379-408.

Scherbaum, C. and Shockley, K. (2015) *Analysing Quantitative Data for Business and Management Students*. London: Sage.

Thompson, B. (2004) *Exploratory and Confirmatory Factor Analysis*. Washington, DC: American Psychological Association.

Williams, L., Ford, L. and Nguyen, N. (2002) Basic and advanced measurement models for confirmatory factor analysis. In S. Rogelberg (ed.), *Handbook of Research Methods in Industrial and Organizational Psychology*. Oxford: Blackwell, pp. 366-389.

INDEX

NOTE: page numbers in *italic type* refer to figures and tables.

Fold a Camel

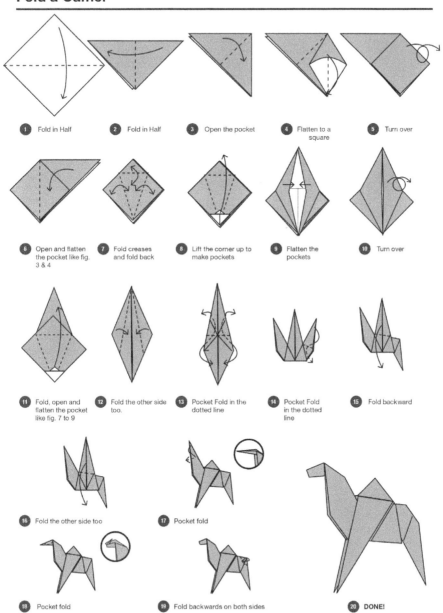

1. Fold in Half
2. Fold in Half
3. Open the pocket
4. Flatten to a square
5. Turn over
6. Open and flatten the pocket like fig. 3 & 4
7. Fold creases and fold back
8. Lift the corner up to make pockets
9. Flatten the pockets
10. Turn over
11. Fold, open and flatten the pocket like fig. 7 to 9
12. Fold the other side too.
13. Pocket Fold in the dotted line
14. Pocket Fold in the dotted line
15. Fold backward
16. Fold the other side too
17. Pocket fold
18. Pocket fold
19. Fold backwards on both sides
20. **DONE!**